This book tells the story of England in a unique way, th[...] and colourful inn signs with hundreds of phot[...]

Read how each sign is a work of art in its own right; it represents a small piece of England's history, its cultural, political and scientific achievements, its heroes and villains, its personalities both real and legendary, and its ancient customs and folklore.

The first 'official' inn sign, the White Hart, was the emblem of King Richard II.

Take a random tour of England, through London, the picturesque cathedral cities, old market towns, quaint little villages and places of scenic beauty. Visit its heritage of inns and experience first hand the atmosphere of those special places where history was made.

The Hart of England is a must for everyone who loves England; a keepsake, an attractive souvenir, an ideal gift, a true treasury of this nation's heritage.

MELROSE
BOOKS

The Hart of England

The history and culture of England told through its inn signs

By Pete Coxon

Photographs by Pete Coxon and Alan Wilson

Published by

MELROSE BOOKS

An Imprint of Melrose Press Limited
St Thomas Place, Ely
Cambridgeshire
CB7 4GG, UK

www.melrosebooks.com

FIRST EDITION

Copyright © Pete Coxon 2011

The Author asserts his moral right to be identified
as the author of this work

Photographs by Pete Coxon and Alan Wilson
Cover design, typesetting and art direction by Matt Stephens

ISBN 978 1 907732 26 3

Printed and bound in China by Latitude Press

No pilgrims now, but tonsured men of grey
Still seep through walls to haunt the shallow light.
No smugglers, no more highwaymen, their prey
The coachmen, long lost in the moonless night.

The humble blacksmith's arms beside his lord's
Still proudly stand where smithy stood before;
White Hart, Red Lion, Crown and chequered boards
The fugitive's Royal Oak, the King's Blue Boar.

Our heritage carved out in English stone
Of weathered Lakeland grey and Cotswold gold;
Thatches and timbers Englishmen have grown
To frame their signs of arms emblazoned bold.

Come drink with me, and celebrate again
Our inns, the pride of all good Englishmen!

Sections

The English Inn

The Rose & Crown, *Snettisham*

Near yonder thorn, that lifts its head on high,
Where once the sign-post caught the passing eye,
Low lies that house where nut-brown draughts inspired,
Where grey-beard mirth and smiling toil retired,
Where village statesmen talked with looks profound,
And news much older than their ale went round.

Oliver Goldsmith, *The Deserted Village*

In the Norfolk village of Snettisham, not far from
the royal residence of Sandringham, stands an ancient
white-walled inn known as the Rose & Crown.
Some two hundred years ago its morning tranquillity
would have been broken only by the Royal Mail
coach from London to Wells-next-the-Sea, arriving
here each day at precisely thirteen minutes past eight,
rattling through the rolling farmland hills at the
formidable speed of ten miles an hour and stopping
only long enough to change horses every ten or
fifteen miles. The returning coach would call here

at five thirty-five each evening on its fifteen-hour journey back to the Swan with Two Necks or the Bell & Crown in London.

Unlike many old inns, the Rose & Crown has no spectacular views of mountains, lakes or riverside. It does not look out onto old street-markets, medieval castles or towering cathedrals. It boasts no famous visits from kings, nobles or other noteworthy Englishmen. It claims no part in the shaping of English history, although we shall visit many such notable hostelries in this book on our journey through England's history and culture, where we can sit where the bowmen of Agincourt and sailors of Trafalgar once sat, enjoying our refreshments as they did in bygone days.

The Rose & Crown is the typical village inn, a piece of old England, a treasure of a kind to be found nowhere else in the world. Built in Old Church Lane in the fourteenth century to provide food and shelter for the medieval masons and carpenters constructing the village church, the inn, set amongst flowering plants and shrubs, regularly wins awards for its hospitality. Its walled flower garden was once a bowling green. The log-fired interior is full of old beams, winding corridors, uneven stone floors and quaint old bars and restaurants. Up the very steep and narrow stairs are guest rooms with such names as the Old Blue Room, The Staircase and The Chimneys. It is the archetypal English country inn.

The Rose & Crown, Salisbury

Its name is not unique; it is popular throughout England and marks the end of the Wars of the Roses in 1487 and the beginning of the Tudor dynasty, the transition from medieval England to the English renaissance. The sign at Snettisham bears a yellow rose; most bear a red one. The one in Salisbury, a thirteenth-century Rose and Crown, with fine views over the river Avon across the fields to Salisbury Cathedral, shows a red rose within a white one. The Rose & Crown at Kew shows the true Tudor Rose, the white inside the red, representing the marriage of Elizabeth of York to Henry VII which unified the houses of York and Lancaster and promised to bring peace to the land.

The Rose & Crown, *Kew*

In contrast to Snettisham's quiet country inn, the ancient Angel & Royal stands majestically overlooking the old market square in the town of Grantham, birthplace of one-time Prime Minister Margaret Thatcher. It was described by Ted Bruning in his *Historic Inns of England*, published in 2000, as one of England's most important inns, both historically and culturally. Standing 107 miles north of London along the Great North Road, in the great coaching era it was the stopping place for the Edinburgh mail at 7.23 each morning, almost twelve hours after setting off from the Bull & Mouth in London's St Martin le Grand.

The Angel & Royal, *Grantham*

Listed in Roger Protz's *Britain's 500 Best Pubs*, it is built on the site of an Anglo-Saxon manor belonging to Queen Edith. It probably became an inn during the twelfth century, the word inn being derived from an old Saxon word for 'chamber'. As with many old inns, it claims to be haunted. Staff and guests claim to have seen a ghostly white lady in the bedrooms and corridors of the second and third floors. In its own leaflet describing its fascinating history, The Angel & Royal claims to be England's oldest inn with a 600 year-old façade. Two hundred years before, an older inn stood here, belonging to the Knights Templar until their infamous suppression in 1312. The masonry in the cellar is from the Templars' time.

The entrance was built in preparation for a visit by Edward II. It leads to an interior full of character with two hotel bars, The Falcon and The Angel, and the well-preserved King's Room Restaurant in which Richard III held court. Other notable royal guests have included King John of Magna Carta fame and the unfortunate Charles I. The inn was originally The Angel – the 'Royal' epithet was to commemorate a visit from Edward VII, then Prince of Wales, in 1866. A suggestion to call it The Royal Angel was turned down as it was said that the Prince was royal but no angel.

The English innkeeper in centuries gone by was a man of considerable status. It was his role to provide clean comfortable beds and good food, wines and ales to the well-heeled traveller. He would employ brewers, cooks, many serving maids and ostlers to take care of the horses.

*The **Old Thatch Tavern**, a half-timbered thatched pub, one of Stratford-upon-Avon's oldest hostelries.*

Tavern-keepers, while not providing beds, would also have status and many were prominent members of the community. Most of their customers could afford to eat and drink well. Some taverns sold only wine, well out of reach of a labourer's wages. To preserve the standards of taverns a law was passed in 1533 allowing only forty taverns to operate in London, eight in York, and fewer in other cities and towns.

The Ale House *in Bath. Originally home to a spirit merchant's business it became a small one-roomed alehouse a hundred years ago. Listed in the* Good Pub Guide, *it is now one of the city's best-known bars.*

At the bottom of the scale was the humble English alehouse. That is, until the accession of William of Orange in 1688. Within a few years gin from the Netherlands had become the scourge of the land:

by 1740 eight million gallons a year were being consumed and the influence of gin palaces was badly affecting the nation's productivity, health and family life. Hogarth's famous prints *Beer Street* and *Gin Lane*, published in February 1751, helped to bring about the Gin Act. The Old Poets' Corner in Ashover, Derbyshire is described by the *Good Pub Guide* as "a simple village pub". Its sign bears lines from a poem by the Reverend James Townley, written to accompany the *Beer Street* print:

Beer, happy produce of our Isle,
Can sinewy strength impart
And wearied with fatigue and toil
Can cheer each manly heart

Labour and art upheld by thee
Successfully advance
We quaff thy balmy juice with glee,
And water leave to France

Genius of health, thy grateful taste
Rivals the cup of Jove
And warms each English generous breast
With liberty and love.

Hogarth compared the virtues of drinking English beer with the evils of the continental gin which was destroying English society through addiction to the cheap and widely available spirit popularised by the followers of King William. Gin became known in England as 'Mother's ruin'. In the year that *Beer Street* was published, the Gin Act was passed to impose duties and to control gin sales. The way was clear once more for the Englishman to enjoy his beer and, at this time, most establishments would still brew their own.

The Old Poets' Corner, *Ashover*

Good Luck to the Barley Mow

Ye Olde Barley Mow, Lincoln

A small brick-built terrace pub in Bailgate, in the high part of Lincoln, displays the sign Ye Olde Barley Mow (the 'Y' in Ye being the old way of writing 'Th'). The sign shows farmers and their wives dancing around the barley mow, a heap or stack of barley, beer's main ingredient. The medieval type of barley was then known as 'bere'. Beer was the staple drink in early England as water was usually unfit for human consumption. Little wonder that the barley harvest was cause for celebration, much as the traditional central European Oktoberfest is today.

The Barley Mow became a traditional English drinking song in which participants take a drink at the end of every verse. Sometimes each round has to be sung in one breath with failure resulting in the 'forfeit' of taking another drink. The first verse is often –

Here's good luck to the landlord, good luck to the barley mow,
Jolly good luck to the landlord, good luck to the barley mow,
The landlord, the pint pot, the half a pint, half a gill, quarter
gill, nipperkin and the round bowl,
Here's good luck, good luck, good luck to the barley mow!

A nipperkin is an eighth of a gill and a bowl is the amount of drink held in cupped hands. Characters are added in each verse: the landlady, barmaid, brewer, drayman, company and more, and sometimes other measures of drink such as bushels and gallons are also added to the verse one by one.

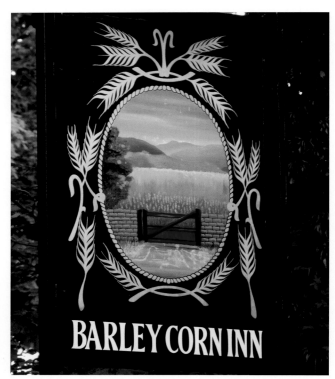

The Barleycorn Inn in Scholes, a village on the outskirts of Leeds

The Two Brewers, *London WC2*

One might imagine the last verses to be a little more slurred than the first, but beer varied in strength, the same mash being used for three or four brews. The final brew, the weakest, known as 'small beer' was reserved for the women and children.

The Two Brewers stands in London's Monmouth Street. Close to Leicester Square and Covent Garden, its small frontage is festooned with hanging baskets and window boxes. Its clientele includes stage personalities and it displays many signatures of actors around the interior walls.

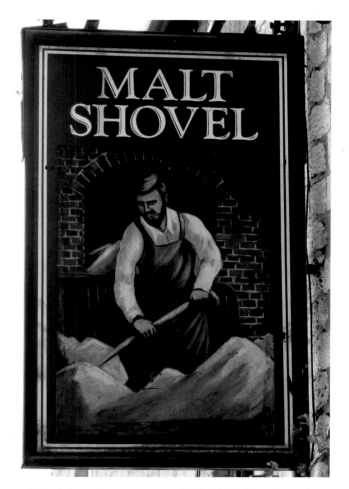

*The eighteenth-century stone-built **Malt Shovel** stands in the North Yorkshire village of Hovingham, home to the Duchess of Kent's Worsley family*

Beer can be produced from any cereal crop but it is normally made from barley and steeped in water for a few days to start germination. It is then heated in a kiln to prevent further growth, turning it into malt, which is crushed to produce grist.

> *Say, for what were hop-yards meant,*
> *Or why was Burton built on Trent?*
> *Oh many a peer of England brews*
> *Livelier liquor than the Muse,*
> *And malt does more than Milton can*
> *To justify God's ways to man.*
> *Ale, man, ale's the stuff to drink*
> *For fellows whom it hurts to think.*
> A. E. Houseman – *A Shropshire Lad*

The grist is mixed with hot water in a mash tun. In England the best water for brewing is from the River Trent at Burton, and many smaller brewers 'Burtonise' their local water supply by adding minerals. Yeast is added to the mash after cooling for the fermentation process. A good brewer values his yeast; each strain is unique and adds its own taste to the brew. He may lodge a sample of his yeast in a yeast bank in case his supply becomes contaminated or dies and his unique flavour is lost forever.

The dark beer known as porter is said to have been invented by mistake by a Covent Garden brewer in the early eighteenth century. Reluctant to pour the burnt-flavoured liquid away, he put it on sale and the local fruit and vegetable market porters lapped it up, hence its name. Some years later, in 1759, the Englishman Arthur Guinness bought a disused brewery in Dublin, and finding it difficult to compete in beer sales he turned to the strong version of porter called stout. The world-famous drink still bears his name.

The sign of the Market Porter hangs outside a pub in Stoney Street in Southwark's Borough Market. The market dates from the thirteenth century when traders moved here from London Bridge. It was closed by Parliament in 1755 but the residents raised £6,000 to buy the present site, once St Margaret's churchyard. The pub pre-dates the market by more than 100 years, but the existing building is more recent, dating back to the nineteenth century. Its old-fashioned interior was made even more so when it became the 'Third-hand Book Emporium' in the film *Harry Potter and the Prisoner of Azkaban*.

***The Market Porter**, London SE1*

***The Porter**, Bath*

A pub in George Street in Bath was once known as the Porter Stores, from the drink it sold. It now displays the sign of a railway porter.

The Golden Lion, *in the picturesque village of St Ives, an artists' paradise in Cornwall*

In his 1994 book *The English Pub*, Peter Haydon tells us how hops were introduced into English beer, probably influenced by Edward III's marriage to his Flemish wife, to satisfy the tastebuds of Flemish weavers who had settled in East Anglia. The queen's personal lion badge was black, but the Golden Lion of Flanders graces many an English inn.

The transition from drinking ale to drinking beer flavoured and preserved by the hemp-related plant was not an easy one, although the preservative helped commercial brewers in producing large quantities which could be stored. Henry VIII banned the use of hops in beer and Haydon tells us that many rural areas stuck by their proper English un-hopped ale well into the eighteenth century.

The Hop & Friar, *in Shrewsbury, Shropshire*

The Belgian Monk, *Norwich*

The Belgian Monk, Norwich

The Three Tuns appears on the coat of arms of the Brewers' Company. In medieval times three real barrels hung outside the English inn, and sometimes a bunch of grapes hanging below would advertise that wine was also sold. It is still a favourite sign.

The Belgian Monk in Norwich's Pottergate perhaps shows that the England of today is more receptive to the Flemish-style brews. These very strong beers were originally brewed in monasteries. They must have been one of the few pleasures in life for the poor celibate religious orders such as the Trappists, who were unable to speak because of their religious vows and perhaps also because of the strength of their brews. The Norwich pub, themed on Grimbergen Abbey, was opened in December 2000 serving forty-five varieties of Belgian beer.

The Three Tuns, Windsor

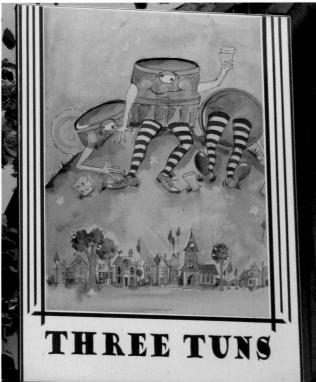

The Three Tuns, *Henley-in-Arden*

The one in Windsor shows the barrels with the famous castle in the background. A plaque outside tells us that the pub was built around 1518 for the town's Trinity Guild and was once the town hall. By the seventeenth century it was also an inn.

On the Three Tuns sign in Henley-in-Arden, Warwickshire, different pictures are displayed on either side of the sign. We are warned of the effects of taking advantage of the English twenty-four hours-a-day licensing laws.

In medieval times, tavern-keepers would serve their last drinks by nine o'clock on summer evenings and eight o'clock in winter, but the innkeeper had to offer twenty-four-hour hospitality to travellers. Later, the only prohibited drinking times were during the hours of divine service, but laws restricting opening hours were reintroduced during the First World War.

A small corner pub in a terraced residential area of Whitby, uphill to the west of the estuary, has the turn of phrase "First in, last out". It is said that this name was often given to pubs on the outskirts of a town. Its inn sign in the small beer garden to the front shows, on either side, one of the landlord's most profitable customers, implying a different meaning to the name.

Job insecurity in Britain gave rise to the phrase "Last in, first out" as those workers most recently employed would find themselves the first to be made redundant. Oscar Wilde's words "Work is the curse of the drinking classes" offer some comfort to those losing their jobs.

On the corner of North Street in Grantham stands the Nobody Inn, aptly described in the *Good Pub Guide* as "a bare boards open plan local with five or six good ales". The sign seems to justify its inclusion among England's best hostelries, with its satisfied customers keeping the secrets of its hospitality to themselves.

First In Last Out, *Whitby*

Nobody Inn, *Grantham*

According to Dunkling and Wright in their 1987 *Pub Names of Britain*, the sign of the seventeenth-century Hoop and Grapes in London's Aldgate High Street was once probably the Hops and Grapes, a bunch of grapes garlanded with hop leaves. A wreath of hops on a pole was once a sign that freshly brewed beer was ready for tasting. Built in 1598 as the Castle, the old inn survived the Great Fire of 1666. After the fire, timber-framed construction was banned in London and this claims to be the only one left in the city.

The English inn sign probably dates from Roman times. Throughout the Roman Empire the sign of the vine leaves, symbolic of the Roman god Bacchus (the Greek equivalent being Dionysus) was used to denote their wine *tavernae*.

After the Romans had become accustomed to wine they began to regard beer as the drink of barbarians, the wearers of beards and trousers. The Roman senator and historian Tacitus wrote in the first century AD that, "The Teutons have a horrible brew made from wheat or barley." The occupying Roman forces, probably the first strangers to travel extensively through England, needed signs to show them where to drink wine and where to avoid the dreaded barbarian brews.

The Hoop & Grapes, *London EC3*

The Grapes, *Bath*

The Grapes of Bath displays a typical modern sign. The frontage in Westgate Street dates from about 1720, but other parts of the inn are said to be from Tudor times. In 1776, under the name of the Bunch of Grapes, it held a wine licence but some fifty years later it also sold beer there in addition to what it described as its "excellent wine and spirit trade".

The Grapes, *Falmouth*

The Grapes overlooking Falmouth harbour displays a sign which, had it been there in Roman times, would have been the cause of many sore heads under the crested Roman helmets. The image is of Bacchus, with the vine leaves of the old Roman inn sign adorning his hair.

The Grapes Tavern, *an early nineteenth-century pub in the heart of Hereford. The view shows the cathedral and the old Wye Bridge.*

The original version was painted by the gifted but notorious Italian artist Michelangelo Merisi da Caravaggio in about 1595 and shows a teenage boy trying to hold up his glass of wine, while obviously suffering from its effects. The Grapes sign turns the figure of Bacchus back into a classical horned and bearded demonic character, with fresh grapes and vine leaves replacing the wine and the display of fruit which looks to be well past its sell-by date. Caravaggio's work, painted when he was aged about twenty-five, can be seen in Florence's Uffizi gallery.

From a popular inn name to one claiming to be unique: the Comus in Camblesforth, east Yorkshire, a large country inn a few miles to the south of Selby. Inside are photographs of the building before it was converted from a farmhouse. It also displays a photograph of a warship, the corvette HMS *Comus*, dated 1895. For many years ex-crew members would travel from all parts of the country for reunions here, until they were too old and too few. Some thought the inn to have been named after the ship.

In fact it is named after the legendary god of hospitality, translating from the Greek *komos* as revelry. The son of Bacchus and Circe, he was also the god of festivity, excess and nocturnal dalliances, representing chaos. During the festivals in his honour in ancient Greece the men and women would change clothes. This inn sign depicts him as an old man, but in ancient times he was usually portrayed as a young man wearing a flowery wreath on his head and being on the point of collapse through drunkenness and about to drop his fiery torch.

The Comus, *Camblesforth*

John Milton wrote his masque *Comus* in baroque style, telling the story of a lady lost in the woods and rescued from Comus by her two brothers. Written for a private showing, it was first performed in 1635 at Ludlow Castle.

Milton campaigned for religious freedom against the Church of England and against the strict Puritans, both of which he believed restrained the expression of personal beliefs. Having praised the execution of

Charles I, he was lucky to survive the Restoration of the monarchy, and he lived on to complete his most famous works, *Paradise Lost* and *Paradise Regained*.

A short walk from the castle, built outside of the gates to the old St Laurence's church, is The Church Inn. In medieval times churchwardens had the responsibility of brewing ales to sell at 'Ale frolics' raising church funds. There were attempts to ban the practice in 1603 and some fifty years later, during the Commonwealth, it was effectively discontinued.

The Church Inn, Ludlow

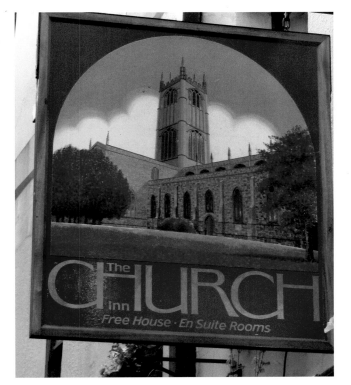

The Church Inn, Ludlow

The inn was recorded in 1446 as belonging to the Palmers' Guild, which was founded in the thirteenth century and endowed three chaplains in the town to pray for the dead as well as providing church music, almshouses and a school. For most of its life the inn was known as the Cross Keys. Its sign is different on each side. One shows the church, the other is of a stained-glass window populated by contemporary local characters including Mitch the flute player, who can be heard playing close to the inn.

First Signs

The Aboard Inn, Appleby

Chequered board signs have been found in the ruins of Pompeii, the Roman town destroyed by ash and lava from Vesuvius in the Bay of Naples in AD 79. It has been suggested that this was the sign of an inn, but the sign might well have been of a counting house where the chequered board was used, or even a gambling den where draughts or chequers were played.

The game is shown on the sign of the Aboard Inn in Appleby, Cumbria, the former county town of Westmoreland, famous for its horse fairs set up by Royal Charter in 1685. Held each June, the fairs attract thousands of horse-trading and fortune-telling gypsies, many in colourful horse-drawn caravans, from all over Britain.

***The Board & Elbow**, Penrith*

in about 1900. The bar, or "snug", attached to the brewery became known as the Elbow Room, probably because of the lack of space, and a medieval armoured elbow now supports the sign. The inn incorporates the Old Black Lion next door, an inn dating from 1624.

***The Chequers**, Sutton in the Isle, Cambridgeshire*

In nearby Penrith, the Board & Elbow shows a similar theme. A notice board at the inn tells us that in the mid-seventeenth century it was known as the Gambling Corner House, but that was because the tailor who had his corner shop there bore the name of Mr Gambling. It later became a wine and spirit merchants before being bought by the local brewery

Across the Pennines, in the High Street of the Yorkshire town of Knaresborough (pronounced 'Naires-bro'), the old inn dating from 1639 shows an unusual interpretation of the board sign.

The Board Inn, *Knaresborough*

A board of company directors in regency-style costume ponder over the fortunes of their venture.

The Chequers *in Bilton, North Yorkshire*

The chequers sign became more popular during the reign of Edward VI (1461-1483). It was on the arms of the Fitzwarren family, responsible for the licensing of alehouses.

The White Hart

The White Hart, *Ashby de la Zouche, Leicestershire*

This royal throne of kings, this sceptred isle,
This earth of majesty, this seat of Mars,
This other Eden, demi-paradise,
This fortress built by Nature for herself
Against infection and the hand of war,
This happy breed of men, this little world,
This precious stone set in the silver sea,
Which serves it in the office of a wall
Or as a moat defensive to a house,
Against the envy of less happier lands
This blessed plot, this earth, this realm, this England

The words are uttered by the dying John of Gaunt in Shakespeare's *Richard II*. In the same act he describes his nephew the King as "landlord of England".

In 1393 King Richard II made it compulsory for publicans to display their sign – "Whoever shall brew ale in the town with intention of selling it must hang out a sign, otherwise he shall forfeit his ale." His own badge was the White Hart, a sign that was to become associated with many of England's best inns. Sometimes, as in the case of The White Hart in Ashby de la Zouche, a collared hart is shown. Alexander the Great was supposed to have captured a pure white stag and placed a gold collar around its neck. The White Hart badge was also adopted by Henry V and Edward IV.

The White Hart, *Moretonhampstead, Devon. Above the main door a sign says "Established in the reign of His Majesty King George I (1714-1727)".*

The White Hart, *Appleby, Cumbria*

The White Hart, *Launceston, Cornwall, an eighteenth-century coaching inn*

The White Hart, *Stow on the Wold, Gloucestershire*

The White Hart, *Swaffham, Norfolk. It stands on the site of the Blue Boar which was destroyed by fire in 1775.*

The White Hart Royal Hotel in Moreton-in-Marsh also shows the royal crown and coat of arms. The coat of arms here is that of Edward III, the lions of England quartered with the French fleur-de-lys to demonstrate his claim to the French throne. The Gloucestershire inn has a Tudor room on the ground floor with an open hearth, and more ancient craftsmanship was discovered recently

when nineteenth-century wallpaper was removed. At the height of the coaching era it was one of the town's main inns, situated eighty-two miles out of London on the mail route to Ludlow via Oxford and Worcester. The cobbled floor of the entrance hall used to be the passage to the coach yard at the rear.

A ballroom added in the early 1800s was home to a magistrates' court as well as dancing.

It was already a hundred years old when Charles I stayed here in 1644 on his way to Evesham. At this time its carved 'gallows' sign spanned the street. It acquired the name Royal many years later and a landlord displayed a sign in the room where the King had slept.

When friends were few and danger near
King Charles found rest and safety here.

Established in 1403 under the sign of the White Hart, the inn now called the Falstaff was built at a time when thousands of pilgrims travelled to Canterbury. It was one of many inns outside the west gate entrance from London, housing pilgrims arriving after the curfew hour. Being outside the walls, the area in those days was a 'red-light' area, just as Southwark was to London. The name was changed to the Falstaff in 1783 at a time when Shakespearian plays were increasing in popularity.

The White Hart Royal, *Moreton-in-Marsh, Gloucestershire*

The English Bard

The Falstaff, St Dunstan's Street, Canterbury

The fat, cowardly knight John Falstaff appears in three of Shakespeare's plays and is the subject of Verdi's last opera, loosely based on *The Merry Wives of Windsor*. With an unquenchable thirst, he would have felt at home in any inn.

A charming painting hangs behind the reception desk, showing the inn in the winter of 1955 bearing a much larger sign than today's, portraying Sir John. The Falstaff was hit by enemy bombing in the 1942 blitz but survived with its fifteenth-century timbers intact.

Falstaff's creator himself was a casualty of the blitz. From the Shakespeare's Head in London's Foubert Place, William's life-size figure looks out of a window over Carnaby Street, famous for its fashions of the sixties and home to an important street market when the inn was built in 1735. The Bard still has his head, but his right arm is missing, blown off by a wartime bomb. The inn sign is from a portrait by Martin Droeshout.

The inn's first owners were Thomas and John Shakespeare, distant relatives of William. The street sign on the pub is in memory of Major Henry Foubert, who in Victorian times had a riding school in nearby Six Acre Fields.

Shakespeare's mother was Mary, daughter of Robert Arden of Wilmcote, a small village near Stratford-upon-Avon. When she was about nineteen she inherited her father's farm, now a popular visitor attraction known as Mary Arden House. The village also has The Mary Arden inn, with a modern sign having recently replaced a more traditional one.

The Mary Arden*, Wilmcote*

The Shakespeare's Head*, Foubert Place, London W1*

"The Life and Death of Henry surnamed Hotspur" was the sub-title given by William Shakespeare to his play *Henry IV Part I*. The Hotspur pub stands in Percy Street close to Newcastle's Haymarket metro station.

A sign above the door gives us a short history of the building, licensed as The Hotspur in 1872. It tells us that Percy Street is named after Lord Percy, the first Earl of Northumberland, and that his son Henry was nicknamed Harry Hotspur because of his fiery temper and his battles in the border countries against the Scots.

The Mary Arden, *Wilmcote*

The Hotspur, *Newcastle*

Born in 1366 at Alnwick Castle, a location setting for the Harry Potter films, he was knighted at the age of eleven at Richard II's coronation. A legend in his own lifetime because of his youthful good looks and heroic exploits, at the start of the Wars of the Roses he found himself on the wrong side at the wrong time. On 14 August 1408 at Shrewsbury Fields he died under a hail of arrows, pierced through the brain.

During Shakespeare's boyhood, plays were performed in college halls and inn yards. In 1576 the first theatre, simply called The Theatre, opened in London's Shoreditch. It was here in 1580 that he joined the resident troupe, which became known as The Chamberlain's Men. Seventeen years later the lease expired, as had the owner James Burbage three months before. Burbage's sons moved the old timbers across the Thames to Southwark where they built a new theatre, the Globe. It was then that Shakespeare wrote his play *Henry V*, which began by the Bard encouraging his audience to let their imaginations run wild.

A kingdom for a stage, Princes to act,
And monarchs to behold the swelling scene…
Can this cockpit hold the vasty fields of France,
Or may we cram within this wooden O
The very casques that did affright the air at Agincourt?

Wooden seats were provided for those who could afford them, but most stood crowded in front of the stage looking upwards at the players in their finery. Called 'Groundlings', their role was to scream encouragement to their English heroes and pour scorn on the villains, adding to the atmosphere and compounding Shakespeare's historical myths.

The Bard's last acknowledged play, written in about 1613, was *King Henry VIII*, which in its final scene celebrates the birth of Elizabeth I.

This royal infant…
Though in her cradle yet, now promises
Upon this land a thousand blessings
Which time shall bring to ripeness.

Shakespeare's last play also saw the last performance in the old theatre. Wadding from a cannon set the thatched roof on fire and the glorious Globe burnt down. Shakespeare retired to Stratford where he died in 1616 on his fifty-second birthday.

A new Globe was built, this one with a tiled roof, but it did not survive the Puritan ban on theatre-going, and the keepers of Englishmen's consciences demolished it in 1644. Almost 230 years later a corner pub was built close by, and from it hangs the sign of The Globe.

The Globe, *London SE1*

In 1970 the American actor and film director Sam Wanamaker set up the Shakespeare Globe Trust to fund the building of a full-size working replica. It was completed three and a half years after his death, using authentic materials of oak, lime plaster and water reed thatch. It became the only thatched building in London, specially treated to pass London regulations imposed after the Great Fire of 1666. Shakespeare's plays are once again performed here, complete with seated audiences and groundlings.

Of Cabbages and Kings

The Hearty Goodfellow, *Southwell*

I am a Hearty Goodfellow. I live at my ease.
I work when I am ready. I play when I please.
With my bottle and glass many hours do I pass,
Sometimes with a friend, sometimes with a lass.

The Hearty Goodfellow, in Church Lane close to
Southwell Minster, displays the sign of a jovial drinker
and another sign with the words of a ballad from about
1850.

I feel I am in love to distraction,
My senses all lost in a fog,
And nothing can give satisfaction
But thinking of sweet Molly Mogg.

This is one of fifteen verses of a frivolous poem
written in the eighteenth century in honour of the
landlord's daughter. The diminutive Alexander Pope
was stranded in his local inn, the Rose at Wokingham,

with three friends, writers John Gay and Jonathan Swift and satirist John Arbuthnot. Outside, a storm raged and their coach was going nowhere. Inside there was little to do except describe their admiration for the fair barmaid Molly, though some say her sister Sally was the prettier. Sadly, the Mogg sisters are long gone, as is the old inn in which they served, and a New Rose with its white rose sign stands on a different site, in Wokingham's marketplace.

The sign of The Generous Briton is displayed in King Street in the Leicestershire town of Melton Mowbray, famed for its pork pies. It portrays the famous John Bull and his bulldog.

***The Generous Briton**, Melton Mowbray*

***Molly Moggs**, London W1*

On the Corner of Charing Cross Road and Compton Street the Fair Molly's sign hangs from an inn that was once the Coach & Horses and now bears her name.

His character was created as the personification of England in 1712 by Dr John Arbuthnot in his anti-war campaign. Nowadays dressed in the regency fashion of the early nineteenth century in his top hat, breeches, tailcoat and Union Jack waistcoat, he is the equivalent of the American Uncle Sam who was invented exactly a hundred years later. Unlike his transatlantic counterpart, a man of some authority, the steadfast

John Bull represents the common country squire who puts the world to rights with a tankard of beer in his hand.

Dr Arbuthnot was a man of many talents – physician, mathematician, satirist and mentor, and the inspiration for his friend Swift's *Gulliver's Travels* – but one of his most challenging tasks was doubtless that of a guardian. In faraway Germany, near the Pied Piper's town of Hamelin, an extraordinary discovery had been made; a wild boy, unable to speak, moving through the forest on all fours eating plants. George I of England, visiting his homeland in Hanover, learned of the discovery and ordered that the boy be brought to London where Dr John was given the role of guardian. Theological questions such as "Does the boy have a soul?" seemed to override the medical issues of the day and interest soon waned in the phenomenon, who became known as Peter the Wild Boy. He was sent away to live in the country.

Arrested as a Scottish highlander in 1745, and later as a Spanish subversive, Peter managed to find his way to Norwich. In Bedford Street, there is a small pub named the Wild Man in his memory. It dates back to Peter's time. Peter died in 1785, an old man probably in his seventies. His gravestone in Berkhampstead, Hertfordshire, in the shade of a dog rose, reads simply:

Peter the Wild Boy

– 1785

***The Wild Man**, Norwich*

Charles John Huffman Dickens was born in Portsmouth on 7 February 1812, son of a clerk in the navy's pay office, the second of eight children. When Charles was twelve, his father was imprisoned for debt. All of the family went with him, apart from Charles who was given work at Warren's shoe-blacking factory. His difficult childhood was the inspiration for his many novels and well-known characters. His works also give us an insight into life in nineteenth-century inns, perhaps the most detailed being *The Pickwick Papers*, more properly entitled *The Posthumous Papers of the Pickwick Club*. It inspired B. W. Matz to write *The Inns and Taverns of Pickwick* in 1921, followed by *Dickensian Inns and Taverns* the next year.

knowledge of science, and consequently of human behaviour and relationships, patronising on their way many of England's famous old hostelries.

The Pickwick Bar, Helmsley

The Betsey Trotwood, London EC1

The club's founder, Samuel Pickwick, appears on the sign of the Pickwick Bar in the North Yorkshire market town of Helmsley. The small fictitious Victorian fraternity created a travelling society to expand their

A lively pub, once the Butcher's Arms and now the Betsey Trotwood, stands in London's Farringdon Road, named after a favourite character from *David Copperfield*. Betsey was the aunt of David's father, a man who died six months before David's birth. Her imposing character makes its appearance in chapter one, startling David's mother. Young Copperfield remarks, "She gave my mother such a turn, that I have always been convinced I am indebted to Miss Betsey for having been born on a Friday." Her personality was inspired by Mary Pearson Strong, Dickens' landlady in Broadstairs, whom he visited many times. Her hotel is now called Dickens House.

Dove Cottage in Grasmere was an inn, the Dove and Olive, before William and Dorothy Wordsworth made it their home in 1799. William wrote in his poem *The Waggoner*:

> *There, where the Dove and Olive-bough*
> *Once hung, a Poet harbours now,*
> *A simple water-drinking Bard…*

His water-drinking habits did not impress Sir Walter Scott, who stayed with him in 1805 on a visit to climb Helvellyn. Scott would take to exercising his horse, but unknown to his host only as far as the nearest hostelry, The Swan.

One morning the two arrived together to hire ponies and the landlord blew Walter's cover, expressing his surprise at the Scotsman's early arrival. The Swan has been standing in the heart of the Lake District for more than 300 years, and was once a major posting house for changing the tired horses pulling coaches along the hilly roads.

The Swan, *Grasmere*

> *The time has come, the Walrus said*
> *To talk of many things*
> *Of shoes and ships and sealing wax*
> *Of cabbages and kings*
> *And why the sea is boiling hot*
> *And whether pigs have wings.*

The nonsense poem comes from Lewis Carroll's *Through the Looking Glass and What Alice Found There*. Born Charles Lutwidge Dodgson on 27 January 1832, son of a clergyman, he attended Rugby school. It was here, some twenty years before he attended, that William Webb Ellis, also the son of a clergyman, is said to have invented the game of rugby by picking up a football and running with it. Dodgson went on to Oxford where he earned a maths degree and met the family of the new dean, Henry George Liddell. Assuming the pen name of Lewis Carroll he wrote *Alice's Adventures Underground* for the dean's daughter, Alice. It was later published as *Alice in Wonderland*, followed up by *Through the Looking Glass*. In later life Alice toured, speaking about the author who made her famous.

The Walrus and the Carpenter stands in Monument Street on the corner of Lovat Lane, close to the monument to the Great Fire of London. Lovat Lane was once called Love Lane when it was a 'red-light' area of London. The pub is themed on Lewis Carroll's Alice.

The Eagle & Child, *Oxford*

The sign of the Eagle and Child hangs outside a pub in St Giles in Oxford. The pub, owned by St John's College, dates from 1650 and its sign is from the crest of the Earls

The Walrus & Carpenter, *London EC3*

of Derby, a noble title dating from 1139. Legend tells that one of the earls had an illegitimate child whom he wished to make his heir. Possibly having read the Bible story of Moses and the basket, he had the child placed at the foot of a tree, as if it had been dropped by an eagle, and arranged for it to be discovered by one of his maids. Taken with the child's tragic beginnings, the Earl's wife agreed for them to adopt it.

Between 1939 and 1962 a group of writers calling themselves the 'Inklings' used to meet here on Tuesday evenings in the Rabbit Room to discuss the books they were writing. Its members included J. R. R. Tolkien, author of *The Lord of the Rings*. The Daily Telegraph, in its list of Seventy Great British Pubs, called it, "One of those pubs that you should visit at least once in your life," and remarked, "If Bilbo Baggins had lived in Oxford this is the pub he'd most likely have frequented."

Another of the Inklings was Clive Staples Lewis, born in Belfast in 1898. After winning a scholarship to Oxford in 1916, he volunteered to serve in the army and arrived in the trenches on the Western Front on his nineteenth birthday. After the war he gained a triple first at Oxford and lectured at Magdalene College from 1925 to 1954. C. S. Lewis is best known as the creator of the seven fantasy novels known collectively as *The Chronicles of Narnia*.

The Witch & Wardrobe, Lincoln

A pub in Waterside North in Lincoln, on an attractive waterfront populated with bevies of swans, bears the sign of The Witch and the Wardrobe, taken from *The Lion, the Witch and the Wardrobe*, part of *The Chronicles of Narnia*, published in 1950. It shows Tilda Swinton, nominated for Best Actress for her part as the White Witch in the 2005 film. Although this episode of the book was the first to be published, *The Magician's Nephew* is the first one in chronological order.

The chronicles tell how four children, Peter, Susan, Edmund and Lucy Pevensie, discover that a wardrobe in the house of an old professor leads to the magical land of Narnia. For a hundred years the land has been under the spell of the White Witch, whom they defeat with the help of Aslan the Lion.

All the World's a Stage

Nell of Old Drury, London WC2

In her day, Eleanor Gwynne might also have been in line for a Best Actress nomination. She is said to have been born on 2 February 1650 close to the Old Bull Inn off London's Strand. Known as Nell, she made a living by selling oranges in Covent Garden and perhaps outside the Drury Lane Theatre where, at the tender age of fifteen, she began her stage career. The Nell of Old Drury in London's Catherine Street is named after her. A plaque outside tells us that there has probably been an inn on this site since 1690 when the Theatre Royal opposite was built. The sign is taken from a painting in London's National Portrait Gallery.

Nell's dancing skills, her comic wit and her energy enthralled Samuel Pepys, and John Dryden wrote characters for her to play. She was beloved by the English nation, and by King Charles II to whom she bore two sons, the elder becoming the Duke of St Albans. On his deathbed Charles told his brother, "Let not poor Nellie starve", and although James II did provide for her, she died within two years and was buried in St Martin-in-the-Fields. Her eulogy was read by the church's vicar, later to become Archbishop of Canterbury. Her legacy to the nation is the Royal Hospital in Chelsea, which she is said to have influenced Charles to build. The hospital was founded in 1682 for the "succour and relief of veterans broken by age and war", and is still famous for its red-coated Chelsea Pensioners.

The Nell Gwynne Tavern, London WC2

In Bull Inn Court, on the site of the old inn, a new one stands named in her honour. A plaque outside tells her story and adds a macabre note: "In 1897 William Terris, a well-known actor of the day, was murdered yards from this spot by a stagehand from the Adelphi Theatre".

It was Oscar Wilde who suggested to Lily Langtry that she should take to the stage. Her premiere was at the Haymarket Theatre in 1881 in *She Stoops to Conquer*, written by his fellow Irishman Oliver Goldsmith. Oscar later wrote *Lady Windermere's Fan* for Lily to demonstrate her acting abilities.

Born in St Helier as Emilie Charlotte de Breton, she acquired the soubriquet 'The Jersey Lily'. An aspiring socialite, she became mistress to several admirers including the future King Edward VII.

A black-and-white corner pub, once known as the Peach Tree, next to Nottingham's Theatre Royal, displays the sign of Langtry's. Lily died in 1929 and is remembered in the song *Pictures of Lily*, recorded and released by the Who in 1967.

Pictures of Lily made my life so wonderful,
Pictures of Lily helped me sleep at night.

Langtry's, *Nottingham*

Sweet Nellie Dean

Nellie Dean of Soho, *London W1*

The first music hall in London, the Oxford, opened in 1861. Music halls were effectively the descendants of the singing room of the Victorian pub, but with an audience slightly better behaved and more attentive, and by the 1880s they had become a popular attraction.

There's an old mill by the stream, Nellie Dean!
Where we used to sit and dream, Nellie Dean!
And the waters as they flow
Seem to murmur soft and low.
You're my heart's desire, I love you, Nellie Dean!
Sweet Nellie Dean!

A pub in Dean Street, London displays the sign of Nellie Dean of Soho. The street is named after a seventeenth-century ecclesiastical dean but Nellie's character is fictional. Her song, composed by the American Harry Armstrong, became the signature tune of music hall entertainer Gertie Gitana. Gertie, born Gertrude Mary Astbury in 1887, became a forces' sweetheart during the First World War and entertained in many military hospitals.

A public house called the Lyceum stands in the Strand on the edge of London's theatre-land. Close by is the Lyceum Theatre, built in 1834. Its name is taken from the ancient Athenian gymnasium and school where Aristotle taught, dedicated to Apollo Lyceus, the wolf-god. In its early years it saw English opera and stage adaptations of Dickens' novels. An earlier Lyceum, dating from 1765 and built on an adjacent site, became the first theatre to be lit by gaslight in 1800.

In 1807 Pall Mall became the first street in the world to be lit by gaslight when thirteen lamp posts were installed. That same year gaslight lit the Golden Lane Brewery. By 1819 lighting was supplied for more than fifty thousand London homes by the Gas Light and Coke Company and the windows of hundreds of small shops in Oxford Street amazed Regency Londoners with their radiance. The lamplighter became a familiar sight, walking the streets at dusk to illuminate cities and towns. He appears on the sign of the Lamplighter in Rother Street in Stratford-upon-Avon, lighting the way for the Regency coach.

The Lyceum, London WC2

Sweet Nellie Dean

The Lamplighter, *Stratford-upon-Avon*

Ancient Guilds

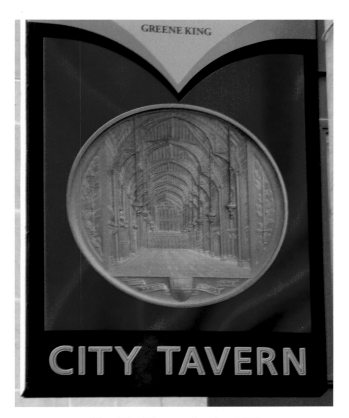

The City Tavern, London EC2

As England and the rest of Europe emerged from the Dark Ages, tradesmen united to protect themselves and their goods from higher authorities at home and abroad, and from outsiders who might seek to compete against them. In England they formed merchant guilds and trade guilds, named from the Anglo-Saxon *gilden* (payment) as they paid subscriptions to their fellowship which would be used to provide charity to members and their familes who had fallen on hard times.

> *There was a merchant with forked beard, and girt,*
> *In motley gown, and high on horse he sat.*
> *Upon his head a Flemish beaver hat;*
> *His boots were fastened rather elegantly.*
> *His spoke his notions out right pompously.*

So Geoffrey Chaucer described the medieval merchant. The wholesale and retail merchants, known in those times as the Mercers, were the wealthiest citizens with powerful monopolies on their goods. In London, theirs was the most senior guild. In large towns Guildhalls were built in which the senior members of each of the guilds could meet together. The merchant guilds would elect a senior spokesman with the title of Lord Mayor, and the senior members representing the guilds would be known as Aldermen. These individuals virtually ran the city's commercial life.

The sign of the City Tavern, in Trump Street, shows the interior of London's Guildhall, which was built nearby in the early fifteenth century above the ruins of a Roman amphitheatre. The great hall, second in size only to the King's Hall, was the scene of Lady Jane Grey's trial and with its Roman ruins is now open to the public.

The Lamb & Flag in James Street, London W1

The Lamb & Flag in Hailey, Oxfordshire

*The **Black Horse**, Elton, Cambridgeshire, once the sign of the London Goldsmiths' Guild in Lombard Street, now adopted by one of Britain's major banks*

London's Guilds were ranked in seniority, with the Grocers and Drapers second and third behind the Mercers. In 1515 the Vintners were ranked eleventh, the Brewers fourteenth and the Innkeepers well behind in thirty-second place. For a time sixth and seventh place was disputed between the Skinners and the Merchant Taylors. The dispute was resolved in 1484 when the Lord Mayor decreed that each should swap places yearly, giving rise to the phrase "at sixes and sevens".

The Merchant Taylors and the Merchant Adventurers are now largely charitable organisations. London charters for both organisations date from more than 600 years ago. The Taylors were originally allied to the Linen Armourers who made the padded tunics to be worn under military armour. Since 1480 their crest has been the Lamb and Flag. Their inn sign normally shows the flag of St George's Cross, but the one in James Street in London shows a Union Flag draped over the lamb. William Blake's poem and hymn *Jerusalem* associates the sacred sacrificial lamb with England's "green and pleasant land".

And did those feet in ancient times
Walk upon England's mountains green
And was the Holy Lamb of God
On England's pleasant pastures seen?

York's Golden Fleece faces towards the ancient street called The Shambles after the benches of the city's butchers who once traded there. It was the inn of the city's Merchant Adventurers. Their trade in medieval times was the export of finished wool, based in England's chief woollen centre outside London. The nearby timber-framed Merchant Adventurers' Hall, completed nearby in 1361, is still a tourist attraction. Until a hundred years ago its undercroft was a hospital caring for the poor and destitute.

The Golden Fleece, London EC4

The Golden Fleece, York

The sign of The Golden Fleece was the ram of Greek legend hunted by Jason and the Argonauts. A halfpenny minted in York, depicting the Fleece sign and bearing the name of landlord Richard Booth, is dated 1668. The sign of The Golden Fleece in Queen Street near London's Guildhall shows Jason with the fleece.

Of London's craft guilds, the earliest recorded was the Guild of Weavers, first mentioned in 1130 although, in terms of precedence, the Mercers' Guild is the most senior. A Weavers sign hangs outside an old medieval house in Canterbury, now converted into a waterside pub and restaurant.

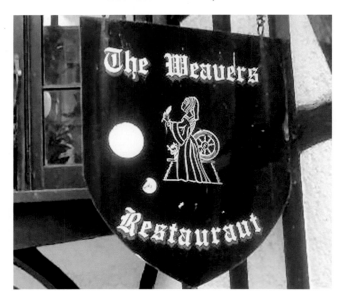

The Weavers, Canterbury.

In the many craft guilds, teenage boys were taken on as apprentices and when they were judged to be experienced enough to work alone they became journeymen, capable of working on their own from day to day for any master. To become a master themselves they would show a 'masterpiece' of their work to the guild fathers, and to preserve the guild's respectability they would also have to provide proof of their wealth and status. Guild masters would ensure that the secrets of their trade were closely guarded and would preside over the religious ceremonies including the annual mystery plays depicting Bible scenes. The word 'mystery' referred to the secret techniques of the crafts, as in Freemasons. The Goldsmiths presented the Adoration of the Magi with their gifts of gold, frankincense and myrrh, while Noah and the Flood was the preserve of Shipwrights and Fishmongers. The Merchant Adventurers, the richest guild, performed the final play, the Last Judgement. In York the tradition of these medieval street performances continues.

In the second millennium BC traders from the eastern Mediterranean visited the south-west of England for the deposits of tin found in the gravel stream beds and in the cliffs. They named the land the 'Tin Islands'. The counties of Devon and Cornwall provided most of the country's tin and copper. Underground mining began in the sixteenth century. At the industry's height 600 steam engines were in use in Cornwall pumping out the mines, but gradually world competition depressed prices. In Cornwall, tin mining has died out but the Cornish pasty, a pastry traditionally filled with meat at one end and apple at the other, reminds us of how the miner carried his lunch to eat underground.

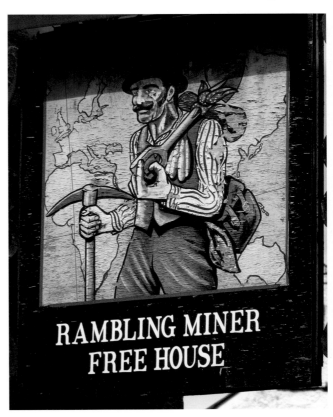

The Rambling Miner, *Chacewater*

The Rambling Miner, in the village of Chacewater, shows the journeyman miner wandering the countryside in search of work.

The sign of The Black Boy probably originated after the Crusades as The Saracen's Head. The sign, in Retford's Moorgate, goes back to one common in the seventeenth and eighteenth centuries on taverns and coffee houses when it was fashionable for the rich to employ negro page boys, dressed in brightly coloured liveries, as personal servants. Sometimes the sign of a black boy was used by tobacconists.

The Black Boy sign in Sudbury, Suffolk takes a different slant. The beamed building on Market Hill is said to date from 1700 and is mentioned in Dickens' *Pickwick Papers*. Here is a cheerful young chimney sweep, but in real life he was hardly the happy, carefree character sung about by Dick van Dyke in *Mary Poppins*.

The Black Boy, *Retford*

The Black Boy, *Sudbury*

How the chimney-sweeper's cry
Every blackening church appalls,
And the hapless soldier's sigh
Runs in blood down palace-walls.

The verse is from the visionary William Blake's *Songs of Experience*, written in 1794. England's impetus in the industrial revolution brought about tall inner-city buildings among Blake's dark satanic mills, tall blocks with taller chimneys. The chimney sweep made his fortune sending soot-covered young orphan boys to climb up inside the blackened and often roasting-hot inner chimney walls, to brush and scrape them clean. Older boys would follow the frightened younger ones, poking their feet with needles to make them climb higher.

Charles Kingsley's book *The Water Babies*, published in 1863, did much to increase awareness of the young sweep's plight and the Chimney Sweepers Regulation Act of 1864 outlawed the use of climbing boys.

London's fashionable mews are now desirable residences for the affluent and famous, but their original purpose was stabling for horses. It was in the beer houses here that servants passed any free time they might have, drinking with their fellows and swapping envious or scandalous tales about the lives and lifestyles of the rich.

Tucked away in Groom Place, a quiet corner of Belgravia, is the unassuming Horse and Groom. In his *London by Pub*, published in 2001, Ted Bruning tells us that it opened in 1864 after the Beer Act abolished beer duty and allowed any householder to sell beer on payment of two guineas a year to the justices. In more recent times it was a local for Beatles' manager Brian Epstein and is still visited by many Beatles' fans.

The Horse & Groom, London SW1

The Bag o' Nails, London SW1

Sporting the prestigious address of 6 Buckingham Palace Road, the Bag 'o Nails was built in the 1830s, replacing an earlier pub. Opinions vary on the origins of its name, perhaps a corruption of Bacchanals, the ancient wine orgies. In *English Inn Signs*, written in 1951, Larwood and Hotten claim that this inn was originally called the Blackmoor's Head & Woolpack but is known locally from its sign as the Devil & Bag of Nails. Another view is that it was the ironmongers' sign. Certainly it was a local for the Buckingham Palace grooms and coachmen, and no doubt for the palace blacksmiths with their pockets full of nails:

> Under a spreading chestnut tree
> The village smithy stands.
> The smith, a mighty man is he
> With large and sinewy hands,
> And the muscles on his brawny arms
> Are strong as iron bands.

The American poet Henry W. Longfellow describes what was once a typical character in every English village and hamlet, a man who would often run the village inn, which would stand next to his smithy. His sign advertised to the traveller that the innkeeper was also the man who could keep his means of transport roadworthy.

The Blacksmith's Arms stands in the Yorkshire market town of Thirsk, a small black-and-white double-fronted pub facing the marketplace. Its location on the Great North Road must have given its eighteenth-century landlord a full purse and tired muscles.

The Blacksmiths Arms, *Thirsk*

Beside the bar is a framed notice dated 1761: "The London-bound coach and four will depart from the courtyard of this inn on Thursday of every week at 11 o'clock in the forenoon, the sum of 50 shillings payable to the coachman. Gentlemen are advised to carry their firearms as a precaution against highwaymen and villains now known to be in the vicinity of Hounslow Heath. Gold, silver and valuables to be placed in the coach strongbox. Many stops for good ale and refreshments twix' here and London."

Around the corner stands the James Herriot Museum, set in the veterinary surgery of the hero of the autobiographical books by James Alfred Wight (using the pen name of Herriot) and the television series *All Creatures Great and Small*. Here the visitor can learn of the skills of the blacksmith, and of the farrier. In bygone days the terms blacksmith and farrier were synonymous but now the authentic farrier combines the expertise of the blacksmith with hoof care and other veterinary practice.

The Farriers Arms, *Worcester*

The Worshipful Company of Farriers tells us that the Celts were the first people to nail metal shoes to their horses' hooves and that horseshoes were used in Britain before the Roman invasion. By medieval times, the practice of shoeing farm horses began and as roads developed the use of horseshoes spread. The Company tells us that in 1356 farriers in the City of London were called together by the mayor and first established as a fellowship. Its modern history begins in 1674 when Charles II granted its first charter.

The Farriers Arms stands in Fish Street, close to Worcester Cathedral. The large inn was once known as the Dark Angel and then the Globe.

As far the English are concerned, the most famous smithy is a few hundred yards across the Scottish border in Gretna Green. It was here that many English couples married, in services performed by the local blacksmith. The 1753 Marriage Act sought to bring marriages in England under the control of church and state forbidding couples under the age of 21 to marry without parental consent. The Scottish lawgivers took the view that marriage was a personal matter. There, couples aged sixteen or over could marry without the consent of others and many sweethearts eloped across the northern border pursued by angry parents.

farriers, saddlers, wheelwrights and coachmen and, as the badge of the House of Hanover, its popularity increased in 1714 when George I became king.

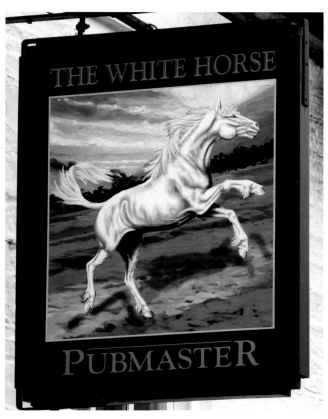

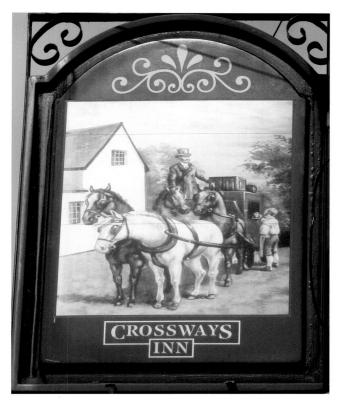

The Crossways Inn, Gretna Green

The Crossways Inn in Gretna Green stands on the crossroads, which couples would pass on their way to the smithy. These days the smithy is still a popular venue for weddings, now attended by familes and friends of the bride and groom.

Since the fifteenth century the White Horse has always been a popular sign, largely because it was adopted by innkeepers as their symbol. It is also the badge of the

The White Horse in Bramham, West Yorkshire

Some inn signs showed that their patrons followed a particular trade, but for anyone who needed the services of a builder it was still safe to enter the Bricklayers' Arms. The Crispin Arms was named after the Shoemakers' patron saint.

The Boot & Shoe, *Tockwith*

The sign of the Boot & Shoe in Tockwith, a village on the site of the Battle of Marston Moor, shows modern footwear; many years ago the boot and shoe was a sign that both local people and travellers were welcome.

An inn called The Golden Slipper stands in York's ancient and narrow Goodramgate, a street dating from Viking times and named after King Guthrum. Parts of this inn date from the fifteenth or early sixteenth century. In 1782 it was known as the Shoe, and by 1818 it had become the Slipper, a sign that it was frequented by local customers, people who lived within a short walking distance and did not need boots for their journey. In 1984 workmen discovered an ancient leather shoe here. There was a medieval custom of placing a pair of shoes in the construction to ward off evil spirits.

The Golden Slipper, *York*

The Globe welcomed visitors from anywhere in the world and was proud of it. The Globe in King Street, King's Lynn, Norfolk was once an eighteenth-century coaching inn on the route between London and Wells. Its sign shows the world borne by Atlas, one of the legendary Titans.

The Globe, *King's Lynn*

The New Globe in Yorkersgate, the main road through Malton, has a more scientific note to its sign. Also a coaching inn, it was the posting house for changing the horses pulling the York to Scarborough mail. There was once an Old Globe inn in the town's marketplace.

The New Globe, *Malton*

Outpost of Rome

The Golden Ball *in York, originally the Roman city of Eboracum. It stands in Victor Street, just inside the city walls.*

The sign of the Globe has an older and deeper meaning. In the year 306, in the Roman city of Eboracum, now known as York, Flavius Galerius Constantinus was proclaimed the new Augustus. He would later become Rome's first Christian Emperor, the founder of Constantinople, and become known in history as Constantine the Great. He soon faced civil war, and on his way to invade Italy in 312 he saw in the sky the Chi-Ro, the superimposed Greek letters symbolising Christ. Sensing divine intervention, he had his soldiers paint the symbol on their shields and they marched on to victory at the Milvian Bridge. A hundred thousand men from the armies of Britain, Gaul and the Rhine defeated twice their number of Italians and Africans. The one bridge into Rome collapsed under the weight of the fleeing enemy, drowning their commander and leading to horrendous casualties among those trapped the wrong side of the river.

Henceforth Constantine took as his symbol the orb, representing his worldly empire, surmounted by the cross of Christianity. Today the emperor's emblem, the sign of the Golden Ball, can be seen on many an English inn.

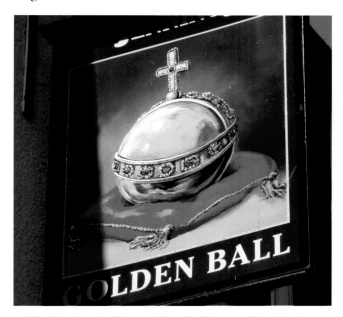

The black-and-white **Golden Ball** *in Appleby, Cumbria*

Broadly speaking, the occupied area of England and Wales was known to the Romans as Britannia, with Scotland and Ireland being called Caledonia and Hibernia. Britannia's personification appeared as a reclining figure on Roman coinage in the second century AD, but the one now familiar to us on the reverse of some fifty pence coins dates from Charles II's reign.

Representing Great Britain and her empire, she also appears on the sign of the Britannia in Chacewater in Cornwall. The King's mistress Frances Stewart, who later became Duchess of Richmond, was the model. Samuel Pepys' diary entry for 25 February 1667 describes her as "The King's new medal… a pretty thing it is, that he should choose her face to represent Britannia by."

The Britannia, *Chacewater*

The Rolling English Road

Ye Olde Watling, London EC4

Before the Romans came to Rye
Or out to Severn strode
The rolling English drunkard made
The rolling English road

G. K. Chesterton's poem describes the winding roads of ancient Britain before the first century AD. Much of Rome's success can be attributed to road-building skills, providing straight, fast communications and manoeuvrability for its armies. One of the most famous in England is Watling Street, running from Dover through London and on to Wroxeter in Shropshire.

In Watling Street in London, leading to St Paul's Cathedral, stands a black and gold-fronted brick-built pub bearing the name Ye Old Watling. A plaque outside describes Watling Street's route and the pub's history. It tells how the pub was built by Sir Christopher Wren in 1668 to house the workers who were rebuilding the cathedral following the Great Fire of London and how it was constructed from the straight lengths of brine-pickled timber of old ships.

Far from the crowded city of London, a remote Northumberland pub stands on the military road close to Hadrian's Wall and the Roman sites of Vindolanda and Housteads, but it is named after an event in the eighteenth century.

The Twice Brewed Inn, Bardon Hill, Northumberland

During the 1745 rebellion General Wade blamed his failure to intercept the Jacobite recruitment march on the condition of the road between Newcastle and Carlisle. Work began to improve the road in July 1751, three years after his death. This inn, halfway between the two cities, was used to house the road builders. They complained of the poor quality beer and demanded that it be brewed again. Strangely, the Twice Brewed Bitter is one of the least potent of the wide range of beers on sale at the inn. Close by there is a youth hostel known as the Once Brewed, opened by the teetotal Lady Trevelyan who said she hoped no alcohol would be consumed there and that the coffee and tea would be brewed only once.

In York's Market Street is a pub which began life in 1843 as the Burns Coffee House, replacing an earlier coffee house of the same name run by Scotsman William McLaren. After a refurbishment in 1985 it was renamed The Hansom Cab.

The Hansom Cab, York

The cab's inventor, Joseph Aloysius Hansom, was born in York in 1803 and became a joiner to follow his father's occupation. Displaying an aptitude for technical design, he later became an architect. In 1834 he patented a design for the Hansom Safety Cab, so-called because of its low centre of gravity. It was also safe in terms of the driver securing payment for his work. Passengers paid him through a trapdoor in the roof, after which he released the door using a lever by his seat to allow them out. A full-size Hansom Cab, built in Birmingham in about 1890, can be seen in the Victorian street of Kirkgate in York's Castle Museum.

In Knaresborough's Market Square stands an eighteenth-century brick building known as Blind Jack's. Its central mock windows are delightfully painted with Blind Jack leaning out of the top floor playing for the children below.

Its name honours John Metcalfe, who was born in Knaresborough on 15 August 1717. Blinded by smallpox at the age of six, he could find his way through the town at the age of nine, and as a robust young man standing six feet tall, an unusual height for those days, he had become an accomplished fiddler playing at country dances. He fled his native town after fathering an illegitimate child, first to an aunt's home in Whitby before spending time in London and Newcastle, then returning home and marrying a local girl. He later

joined King George's army to fight against the '45 rebellion and played his music at a country dance ball in Edinburgh. After the wars he began to operate a wagon service between Knaresborough and York, and embarked on a thirty-year career of road-building. He is said to have been responsible for the construction of about 180 miles of road, which earned him a small fortune before he died at the ripe old age of ninety-two. The inn sign shows his viameter, a road-measuring device which he could read by sense of touch.

Blind Jack's, *Knaresborough*

Blind Jack's, Knaresborough

A Ribbon of Moonlight

The George, London SE1

Featured in practically every book on English inns, The George in Borough High Street is London's only remaining galleried coaching inn. On a sunny summer's day, sitting in the old coaching yard, it is easy to imagine those bygone days. *The London Pub* by Haydon and Coe, published in 2003, says "Without a shadow of doubt, the George Inn is the most important pub in London."

The old pub, frequented by Shakespeare thanks to its proximity to the Globe Theatre, was destroyed by fire in 1676. A new one was built and at the height of the coaching era the George served eighty coaches a week and countless private carriages. The old inn features in Dickens' *Little Dorrit*. It bears the old crusaders' sign of St George.

England's coaching era is generally accepted to have started in 1657 when the Chester coach was inaugurated, and within twenty-five years public coaches were in general use. Road improvements towards the end of the eighteenth century paved the way for the building of faster coaches and more comfortable travel.

The wind was a torrent of darkness among the gusty trees,
The moon was a ghostly galleon tossed upon cloudy seas,
The road was a ribbon of moonlight over the purple moor,
And the highwayman came riding,
Riding, riding
The highwayman came riding, up to the old inn door.

Alfred Noyes' poem *The Highwayman* romanticises the eighteenth-century horseman who was, in reality, a robber and murderer who preyed at night mainly on lone travellers. Occasionally he would hold up a coach full of passengers if he could be sure that none of them was armed. The villain would often work in league with an innkeeper who might assess the contents of his customer's purse before passing on information about the unfortunate victim's wealth and route.

The sign of The Highwayman in Sheriff Hutton in North Yorkshire shows our courageous dashing hero having disposed of soldier and civilian alike, leaving the scene of his crime with the lady's honour intact but her jewels calmly taken from her. The inn dates from about 1780 but an earlier inn on this site was said to have been visited by Richard III when he was staying at the village's medieval castle. Until the 1950s the inn had the less romantic name of the Pack Horse.

The Highwayman, *Sheriff Hutton*

The Dick Turpin in Woodthorpe, York

Of all of England's highwaymen the most notorious was Dick Turpin, immortalised in Harrison Ainsworth's novel *Rookwood*, published in 1834. Outside The Spaniards Inn in Hampstead, a board gives a long history of the inn and tells us that it was here that Turpin was born in 1705. It was supposed to have been from here that he planned his hold-ups of coaches carrying wealthy travellers. It says also that Keats wrote his *Ode to a Nightingale* here, that it is

mentioned in the novels *Pickwick Papers* and *Dracula*, and that it was visited by Goldsmith, Byron and Sir Joshua Reynolds.

The Spaniards Inn, Hampstead

Disappointingly, Turpin was not the loveable rogue celebrated in the old song *Oh Rare Turpin Hero* nor the adventurer portrayed in *Rookwood*. His legendary ride to York on his horse Black Bess to create an alibi for his crimes was probably performed by a robber called John Nevison. As a teenager, Turpin was apprenticed to a Whitechapel butcher, but after some cattle stealing he fled from the law to Epping Forest where he joined the notorious Gregory Gang, a group of violent housebreakers. Most of the gang were executed but Turpin escaped. He was eventually caught for horse stealing and murder and executed in York in 1739, calmly speaking from the gallows to those who had come to watch his demise. His body lay in the cellar of the Blue Boar (now the Little John) in York awaiting burial as the landlord charged his customers to venture downstairs to view the corpse. It was excavated shortly after burial, placed by body snatchers on a surgeon's doorstep and paraded through the town by the mob. At last Turpin had become the heroic figure of legend. The authorities recovered the body, and covered it in quicklime before reburial to make it useless for medical research.

By the early 1780s the highwayman's days were numbered and the chilling call of "Your money or your life" was seldom heard in the dark and lonely night. Roads were becoming faster and wider, affording less cover for the stealthy robber. The arrival of Royal Mail coaches in 1784 with their armed guards and locked strongboxes practically ended the prospect of rich takings.

Over the cobbles he clatters and clangs in the dark inn-yard;
He taps with his whip on the shutters, but all is locked and barred;
He whistles a tune to the window, and who should be waiting there
But the landlord's black-eyed daughter,
Bess, the landlord's daughter,
Plaiting a dark red love-knot into her long black hair.

By 1800 the golden age of coach travel had arrived and the next three decades saw the development of the British Royal Mail. At a speed of ten miles an hour and changing horses every ten or fifteen miles, the 200-mile journey from London to York was cut from four days to less than twenty-one hours. The finely-tuned system was the envy of Europe. What a sight it must have been to see twenty-eight mail coaches leave London's General Post Office every evening at precisely eight o'clock, each journeying to a different destination!

Three of these routes rolled into Wales and three into Scotland, including the longest, to Thurso, taking just over four days. One of them took twenty-two hours to cover the 204 miles to Woodside where the ferries across the River Mersey, made famous in a song by Gerry and the Pacemakers, unfurled their sails every half-hour to carry passengers and mail over to Liverpool.

The sign of an inn close to the site of the Woodside ferry, The River View, shows the famous ninety metre-tall Royal Liver (pronounced Ly-ver) building across the Mersey at Pier Head, considered by some to be the world's first skyscraper. It was completed in 1911 and its clocks were started up at the exact moment of Edward VII's coronation. Perched on top are two mythical cormorant-like liver birds, cast in bronze, guarding the city and its river. Legend has it that if they fly away the city will be destroyed, but fortunately for Liverpudlians they seem to be securely chained to the towers.

The River View, *Woodside*

In the city's Old Post Office Place hangs the inn sign of the Old Post Office, a reminder of the coaching days two hundred years ago.

The Old Post Office, *Liverpool*

The sign of The Bugle, in the Cornish village of the same name, shows the two-ton Royal Mail coach in its black and maroon livery with scarlet wheels. The coach bears the royal coat of arms on its doors, and under its side windows are the insignia of the Orders of the Bath, the Garter, the Thistle and St Patrick. The bugle was originally the horn of a wild ox, used as a drinking horn. The name became used for a hunting horn, and also in some parts of England, a coach horn.

The Bugle Inn, *Bugle*

The Trumpet Inn *at Trumpet, a black-and-white inn at a Herefordshire crossroads dating from about 1456*

The complex network of cross-country mail routes made strict timekeeping essential and even the marching red-coated army columns would have to give way to the sound of a coach horn. It was the guard, a post office employee, who would blow the horn, usually to alert the turnpike-keepers to open their gates to each stretch of road, along which his coach passed free of charge. He also carried a blunderbuss and a brace of pistols to protect the mail box, and never left his seat though his journey might be up to sixty miles long. Next to him, the more fortunate driver, supplied by a contractor, would leave his coach to partake of a tipple at every inn where the horses were changed.

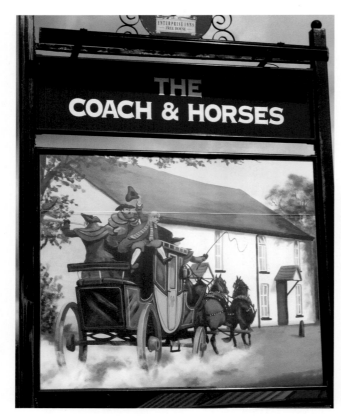

The Coach & Horses, *Spennymoor*

The sign of The Coach & Horses near Spennymoor, County Durham, lies close to the Edinburgh route and shows a privately operated coach, taking longer than the mail coach but offering more passenger comfort by stopping overnight at a welcoming inn. Its colours were quite common and became known as the Devil's Livery – yellow for quarantine and black for death.

The famous stone-built The Old Down Inn at Emborough in Somerset dates from 1640 and stands on a T-junction on the route of the London to Devonport mail which travelled via Devizes, Bath and Exeter. The mail coach on the sign took just under thirteen hours to reach here from the GPO in London, arriving at 8.50 each morning.

The Old Down Inn, *Emborough*

The Coach & Horses in the Oxfordshire town of Banbury, famous for its market cross

The Coach & Horses on the Green, at Adderbury, Oxfordshire, where commercial and private coaches would stop at the turnpike gate, sixty-six miles out of London on the mail route to Stourport

Coaching's golden age was to last only thirty years as the age of rail travel opened up. At first, the new railway carriage would be modelled impractically on the old stagecoach to make the passenger more at ease with the noise and smoke of the new iron horse.

Painted Stations Whistle By

The Rocket, *Rainhill*

Faster than fairies, faster than witches,
Bridges and houses, hedges and ditches;
And charging along like troops in a battle
All through the meadows the horses and cattle:
All of the sights of the hill and the plain
Fly as thick as driving rain;
And ever again, in the wink of an eye,
Painted stations whistle by.

Robert Louis Stevenson's 1885 poem *From a Railway Carriage* scans to the rhythm of the old steam train speeding down the track. In Rainhill the sign of an antique railway engine is displayed outside an inconspicuous brick-built town pub. Over nine autumn days in October 1829 Rainhill, then only a small village nine miles from Liverpool, was host to what has been called the most remarkable event of the industrial age. It became the birthplace of the age of speed. Only four years earlier the world's first

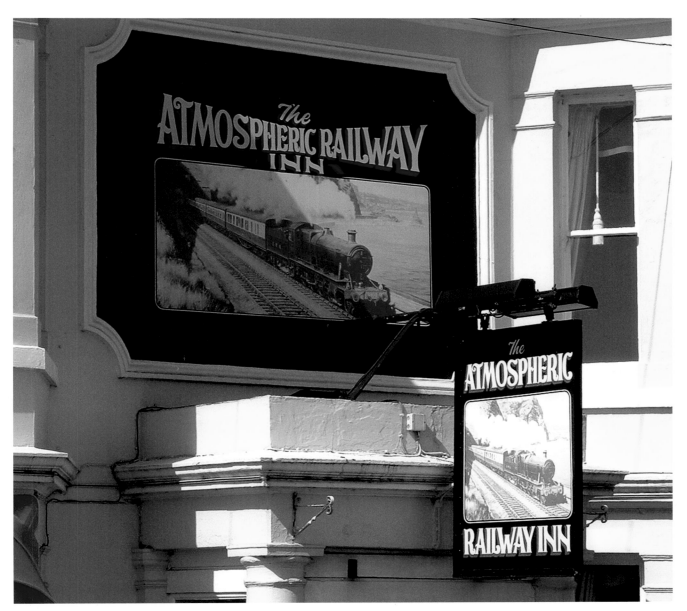

*The **Atmospheric Railway**, Starcross*

passenger train had carried its load along the twenty-seven miles of the Stockton-Darlington railway. The competition at Rainhill was to find the best locomotive for the new Liverpool and Manchester Railway. As the brass bands played, fifteen thousand people, with observers from France, Germany and the United States, watched as the great carnival unfolded.

The five contestants, one of them horse-powered, had to haul twenty tons at ten miles an hour. By the third day only three contestants remained, the crowd's favourite *Novelty*, the *Sans Pareil* and the eventual winner of the £500 prize, the *Rocket*, built by father and son George and Robert Stephenson.

As Prime Minister, the Duke of Wellington attended the railway's grand opening on 15 September the following year, along with William Huskisson, Member of Parliament for Liverpool, who became the first rail fatality as he walked onto the track. At the sight of another approaching locomotive he helped the other passengers back onto his train, but was unable to save himself.

Before the advent of rail travel in Britain the average inhabitant was born, lived and died within a radius of fifteen miles. Within twenty years the British rail network made it possible for the working man to afford to travel from the north to London and heralded the building of railways throughout the world.

With the railway network spreading across England, it was only to be expected that the great Isambard Kingdom Brunel would become involved. More famous for his giant engineering structures and monstrous ships, he also built a broad gauge railway between Plymouth and Exeter. The first section of this, the South Devon Railway, opened in 1846 and three years later it reached Plymouth. The experiment, worked by air pressure, was ultimately a failure and in 1892 the line was rebuilt to the national standard.

At the mid-point of the first section, in Starcross, stands The Atmospheric Railway inn. The village's old pumping station has become the railway's working museum.

The National Railway Museum is housed in York, halfway between the capital cities of London and Edinburgh. As railways took over from coaching, most of York's old coaching inns closed, to be replaced by hotels on the edge of town close to the railway station. Nevertheless, the city still has one of England's best collections of historic inns among its old narrow streets.

The Locomotive, York

The inn sign shows a Jubilee class steam engine, built in the mid–1930s, in the pre-1948 maroon livery of the London Midland and Scottish Railways, carrying passengers cross-country through York. Most passenger trains travelling through the city were pulled by the green-liveried locomotives of the London North-Eastern Railways, such as the *North Eastern* shown on the sign of the Railway Inn in Spofforth, a village between Wetherby and Harrogate.

The Railway Inn, Spofforth

Close to the main London to Edinburgh line is The Locomotive, a suburban pub off Holgate Road, licensed as a beer house in 1848 when it was surrounded by fields. Its first customers would have been the railway's builders, known as 'navvies', an abbreviation of the word navigators. At around this time it was estimated that one in every hundred working men in England was employed in building the nation's railways.

The Railway, *Docking*

The Railway at Docking in Norfolk, a whitewashed pub at the north end of town, was licensed in about 1869. Its sign shows the Western Region Star class 4036 locomotive *Queen Elizabeth*, named after Elizabeth I, built in 1907. The locomotive's design was similar to that of the *City of Truro* built three years earlier, which became the first steam engine to exceed one hundred miles an hour in 1904 on the Plymouth to London run. It was withdrawn from service in 1931 and is now preserved in the National Rail Museum.

The Railway Inn, *in the Cornish town of Launceston*

The Euston Flyer stands outside London's Euston station, the starting point for trains to north-west England and the west of Scotland. The sign seems to show the LMS locomotive Royal Scot class *Cameron Highlander*. Many old steam locomotives were named and also some passenger services, one being the *Royal Scot* running between Euston and Glasgow, but the service's nickname 'Euston Flyer' was unofficial.

The Terminus in the Sussex seaside town of Eastbourne displays the sign of an old 'saddle-tanker' bearing the brewery's name and seems to be based on a model built in about 1932. The high centre of gravity limited the locomotive's speed and it would not normally have pulled a passenger train.

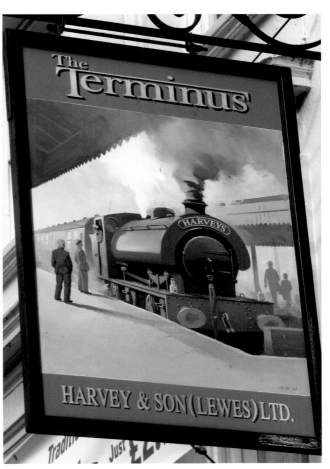

The Euston Flyer, *London NW1*

The Terminus, *Eastbourne*

Waterways of England

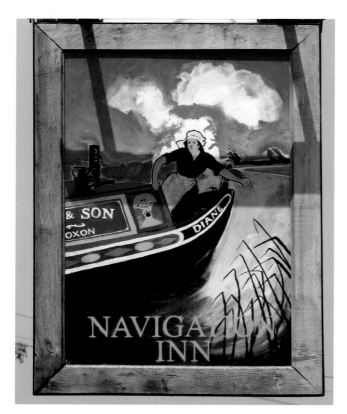

The Navigation Inn, Wootton Wawen

It was not only the coaching trade that was affected by the coming of the railways. The dawn of the industrial revolution had created a need to transport vast quantities of heavy goods such as building materials, coal, grain and finished products and England's muddy, pot-holed roads were simply not up to the task. The canal system was born, a national network stretching from the Thames to the Yorkshire coalfields. Towpaths were built for horses to drag the barges, but in the long dark tunnels men had to lie across the vessels and 'walk' them with their feet against the tunnel walls.

To compete with the railways tolls on waterways had to be reduced and there was little profit. From the 1830s practically nothing was done to improve England's canals and they fell into dereliction. It was only in 1946 that the Inland Waterways Association was founded and voluntary restoration work in the 1960s sparked a new interest – canal holidays. Now the canals are populated by colourful narrowboats and river craft comprising an important part of England's leisure industry.

The Navigation Inn in Wootton Wawen was built about 200 years ago to service the navvies building the Stratford-upon-Avon Canal, which runs through the pub grounds. The twenty-five miles of canal run from Birmingham through the Forest of Arden to Stratford, but its fifty-four locks make the journey about three days long. It was reopened in 1964 by Her Majesty the Queen Mother after restoration.

The Waterman's Arms opened in 1871 to serve the river trade at Osney Lock on a secondary channel of the Thames next to the village that was once the home of the miller in Chaucer's *Miller's Tale*. The lock was built in 1790 by inmates of Oxford prison. The concept of combining a custodial sentence and community service paid dividends, keeping costs down to only £750.

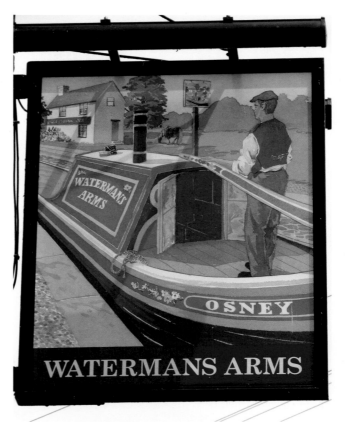

The Waterman's Arms, *Osney*

Once and Future King

The Round Table, London WC2

On either side the river lie
Long fields of barley and of rye
That clothe the wold and meet the sky
And thro' the field the road runs by
To many-towered Camelot.

So Alfred Lord Tennyson, the longest-serving Poet Laureate having succeeded William Wordsworth, describes the way to King Arthur's castle in his poem *The Lady of Shalott.* In the year 1191 the monks of Glastonbury Abbey claimed to have found the grave with the inscription "*Hic jacet Arturus, rex quondam, rexque futurus*" – "Here lies Arthur, the once and future king". The legend of Arthur and his wife Guinevere, her love for Sir Lancelot, Sir Galahad's quest for the Holy Grail used as the chalice at the Last Supper, the wizard Merlin and the magical sword Excalibur, all have been passed down through the ages as the foundation of English chivalry.

Central to the legends is Arthur's fellowship of the round table at which each of his knights sat, no one greater or lesser than any of his fellow knights, the epitome of man's equality to man. The Round Table in London's St Martin's Court displays its sign.

In reality Arthur was probably '*dux bellorum*', the war leader left behind to defend England's fifth-century civilization in battle after the Roman armies had left for Italy, to keep it Roman, to keep it Christian. His tales may have been legend but his battles were real, and for a time he was successful against the Saxon invaders from across the North Sea. Wounded, he was taken to the mysterious Isle of Avalon to be healed. Legend has it that one day, when his country is in grave danger, he will return to fight again.

Built at Exchequer Gate at the top of Steep Hill, Lincoln's The Magna Carta pub is midway between the castle and the cathedral. The pub's interesting interior decor is of light wooden furnishings, swags and twirls, on split levels, modern but with lots of character. Its sign signifies the rights of man.

The Bishop of Lincoln was present at the historic signing of the charter on that summer's day in 1215 and was probably instrumental in the cathedral owning one of the four remaining originals out of forty-one written and given the Royal Seal. There is also a story

The Magna Carta, Lincoln

that the wife of a Lincoln noble, being of Anglo-Saxon blood, was one of the few people who could translate the document's Medieval Latin script into the language spoken by the common man. In recent years the document has been on display in the castle, only a few hundred yards from the pub.

The document comprises about 3,500 words written in tiny black script on vellum, the skin of a calf. It remained in force for only nine weeks before

King John persuaded Pope Innocent III to annul it and the King sent his henchmen to destroy all copies. It was reissued three more times in the next ten years and parts of it still remain today as English law.

The Great Charter benefited the wealthy, but was of little use to the English peasants who made up three quarters of the population. In fact half of them were worse off, 'unfree villeins' from whom the king's protection had been removed. The barons were now free to treat them as slaves and their struggle for freedom would take many years.

> There's no discouragement
> Shall make him once relent
> His first avowed intent
> To be a Pilgrim
>
> John Bunyan, 1684

William Brewster lived in the village of Scrooby in Lincolnshire with his wife Mary, who bore him five children, sons Jonathan, Love and Wrestling, and daughters Patience and Fear. William and his wife, and many of their fellow villagers, belonged to the new 'Separatist' religious movement. Though their leanings were similar to those of the Puritans who aimed to purify the established church, the Separatists believed that Anglicanism was beyond redemption.

The Pilgrim Fathers, *Scrooby*

In 1606 William founded a Separatist congregation in the village manor house, which belonged to the Archbishop of York. Needless to say, he was soon discovered and driven into hiding. The following year the congregation tried to escape to the Netherlands, walking some sixty miles to Boston, where they had chartered a small ship. Betrayed by the captain, they were arrested and imprisoned, but eventually found their way to the Dutch city of Leyden.

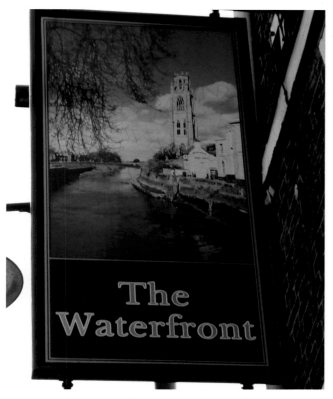

The Waterfront, *Boston, Lincolnshire*

Shown on the sign of The Waterfront in the Lincolnshire town of Boston is the tower of St Botolph's Church, the tallest parish church tower in England, founded in 1309. The tower was completed almost a hundred years before the Pilgrim Fathers sailed. It is affectionately known as the Boston Stump, possibly because it lacks a spire. The name of Botolph's Town became shortened to Boston. Appropriately for the pilgrims, he was the patron saint of travellers before

St Christopher was adopted, and his tower must have been their last sight of Boston on the horizon as it disappeared from view.

Indirectly, Boston in Massachusetts owes its name to St Botolph and the stump. The city boasts America's oldest inn, The Bell in Hand, dating from 1795, named in honour of 'Old Jimmy' Wilson, who was its first landlord and Boston's last town crier.

Given the opportunity of a new life of religious freedom in America, Brewster and his companions, later to become known as the Pilgrim Fathers, left the Netherlands on 22 July 1620 on board the *Speedwell*, which was to accompany the *Mayflower* across the Atlantic. They called at Plymouth to take on supplies. Three hundred miles out into the Atlantic the unseaworthy *Speedwell* was forced to turn back, transferring its cargo and many passengers to the overcrowded *Mayflower*. On 9 November they sighted the New World, and on Christmas Day they began to build the town that was to become the new Plymouth.

Back in England, just across the county border from Scrooby, in South Yorkshire, the village of Austerfield proudly proclaims itself the birthplace of William Bradford, Pilgrim Father. Its inn is called The Mayflower.

The Bell in Hand, *Boston, Massachusetts*

The Mayflower, *Austerfield*

William was born in Austerfield on 19 March 1590, and as a young man attended the Separatist church in nearby Scrooby. Persecuted by James I's regime, William was among the members of the congregation who fled in 1609 to the Netherlands where he married and worked as a weaver. He supported their leader John Robinson in the idea of founding a settlement in America and sailed with his wife on the *Mayflower*. She died while the ship was still at anchor off the American coast, and three years later he married a widow who had sailed from Plymouth in England. After half of the colonists had died in their first year, William was elected as the new governor. He is best remembered for his journal giving an account of the colony's first thirty years.

He was buried at Plymouth Burial Hill, and was the ancestor of many notable Americans including Clint Eastwood, George Eastman, Christopher Reeve and Dr Benjamin Spock.

The Pilgrims' Bar, *Canterbury*

The sign of the Pilgrims' Bar, close to Canterbury Cathedral, makes the connection between Chaucer's pilgrims and those of 1621. It was once part of the Mayflower Restaurant. Both the restaurant and bar have closed but the weather-beaten sign on the whitewashed wall remains.

The Wolfe in Red Clothing

The Wolfe, Penrith

In the Cumbrian town of Penrith stands an inn called The Wolfe. Its sign is of an English hero to whom Canada arguably owes its nationhood.

Born in 1727, James Wolfe was appointed to his father's regiment of marines in 1741, but instead joined the East Suffolk as an ensign. He fought his first battle in Bavaria, at Dettingen, at the age of sixteen and three years later at Culloden is said to have disobeyed an order from the commander, the Duke of Cumberland, nicknamed 'The Butcher', to shoot a wounded highlander.

In 1758 he landed in Halifax, Nova Scotia, with the rank of 'Brigadier in America', and returned the following year to attack the French, who were commanded by the Marquis de Montcalm at Quebec.

'Tis but in vain, I mean not to upbraid you, boys,
'tis but in vain for soldiers to complain.
Should next campaign send us to him who made us, boys,
We're free from pain.
But should we remain, a bottle and kind landlady
Cures all again

The song *Why, soldier, why* was sung by Wolfe and his men on the eve of the battle of the Plains of Abraham. No kind landlady awaited the general. The journey down the dark river, the scaling of the heights and the sad death of both commanders is the stuff boys' adventure stories are made of. James Wolfe was thirty-two when he died, having secured Canada for the British Empire.

The year before his birth, Wolfe's parents lived in a house in York which later became the Black Swan. This fine picturesque building was originally a private mansion owned by the Bowes family. William Bowes was Lord Mayor of York in 1502 and goldsmith Martin Bowes later became jeweller to Queen Elizabeth I.

The Black Swan, *York*

It had become the Black Swan inn by 1763, holding cockfighting in an upstairs room. The fine preserved interior displays many tales of hauntings. Its other claim to fame is the number of celebrities who have visited here and the Canadian servicemen who made it their local during World War II, perhaps subconsciously drawn to where their nation might have been born.

The Wolfe in Red Clothing

These days, a warm welcome is said to await Canadians, and indeed the whole world, at the Maple Leaf in Maiden Lane near Covent Garden. It announces itself as "a small piece of Canada in the Heart of London".

A plaque outside reads "This public house is dedicated to the centuries-old friendship between Great Britain and Canada, and Britons and Canadians. People of all nations are invited within to add to this friendship and to partake of good food and drink with friendly people." Truly the sign of every English inn!

The Maple Leaf, London WC2

Black and White Swans

The Swan was in the arms of Henry V, but the sign of the Black Swan seems to have proliferated shortly after the introduction of a tax on gin in 1736. Landlords of some White Swan inns painted their birds black in protest, creating what was in those times perceived to be a mythical beast. The first real black swans were brought to England by convict ships returning from Australia. But it seems that most signs of the Swan remained white.

The Black Swan in the marketplace of the North Yorkshire town of Bedale. It lies on a route connecting the Great North Road with the Lake District.

The White Swan, Henley in Arden

The White Swan in Henley in Arden, Warwickshire, was built in about 1350. It still retains much of the original structure and was the town's main coaching inn during the early eighteenth century.

The Old Swanne Inn in Evesham, Worcestershire. Close to the town is the site of England's most famous thirteenth-century battle in which, on 4 August 1265, Simon de Montfort, founder of England's first elected Parliament, was slain.

In the small Suffolk town of Lavenham, once famous throughout Europe for its blue woollen cloth, stands the old timbered The Swan. In 1425 the inn was recorded as the home and workshop of prosperous beer-drinking Flemish weavers and two centuries later the clientele were packmen who collected finished cloth around the town. The original part of the inn was on the corner of High Street and Water Street, but gradually the rest of the High Street frontage, then the rest of the block, were incorporated, including the ancient wool hall in Lady Street. A charming garden now forms the centrepiece of the hotel, which retains most of its ancient interior.

An old coaching inn stands in Market Harborough in Leicestershire displaying the sign of the Three Swans, all of them white. It stands on the London to Carlisle mail route that ran via Leicester and Manchester. It is arguably the town's most famous inn, with origins in Tudor times and a frontage dating from 1790. King Christian VII of Denmark dined here in 1768. Its longest-living landlady was Eleanor Seller who died in 1796 at the age of 101. The former coach yard at the rear has been modernised but the building still retains much of the atmosphere of the old coaching days.

The Swan, Lavenham

The Three Swans, *Market Harborough*

After the decline of the coaching era it degenerated into little more than a beer house until it became the third and last inn to be taken over by the eccentric hero John Fothergill, the famous self-proclaimed Amateur Pioneer Innkeeper. His *My Three Inns*, published in 1951, tells of his adventures at the Spread Eagle in Thame, the Royal Hotel at Ascot, and finally here at the Three Swans. His picture hangs in the Fothergill Bar, staring intimidatingly at his contented customers.

Landlords and Rogues

Dirty Dick's, *Bishopsgate, London EC2*

In the busy street of Bishopsgate in London stands another famous old hostelry listed in Roger Protz's *Britain's 500 Best Pubs*. The original site of Dirty Dick's was in Leadenhall Street, and it began life with the grandiose name of the Gates of Jerusalem. It acquired its present name from Nathaniel Bentley (c.1736-1809), once known as the Beau of Leadenhall Street, who inherited his father's business in 1761 when he was a fashionable man-about-town, soon to be married.

Not long afterwards, his fiancée is thought to have died, some say on the eve of their wedding. The devastated young man never recovered from his loss, his fashion sense and cleanliness deteriorated, and he became known by his neighbours as Dirty Dick. They called his hardware shop Dirty Dick's Warehouse and, in spite of their offers to clean the premises, for fifty years he allowed no-one into his private rooms. After

Dick died, the landlord of an inn is said to have bought some of his possessions to attract customers' attention, and renamed his inn Dirty Dick's.

It is doubtful whether Dick was happy with his nickname, but one portly landlord in Devon seems to have had more of a sense of humour. His whitewashed sixteenth-century New Inn in the village of Horndon became known by his customers as The Elephant's Nest. He accepted their sense of humour and renamed the inn officially, erecting a new sign.

The ancient narrow Wansford Bridge seems barely wide enough for a coach and horses to cross. Hard to believe it was once part of the Great North Road on the London to Edinburgh mail route! Across the bridge stands the Haycock, a former coaching inn and now an upmarket country hotel, away from the buzz of traffic now that the A1 follows a different route.

The Elephant's Nest, *Horndon*

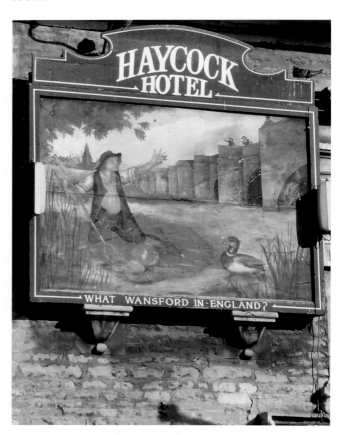

The Haycock, *Wansford*

The hostelry was known originally as the Swan, but by 1712 it had been renamed the Haycock from the legendary Drunken Barnaby who had fallen asleep on a haycock next to the flooded River Neme near Peterborough and floated downstream. He awoke at Wansford Bridge, and on being told his whereabouts he asked, "In England?" hence the inscription on the inn sign. Richard Braithwaite published his *Drunken Barnaby's Four Journeys to the North of England* in 1638, a mixture of Latin and English in doggerel verse. It tells a slightly different version, with the haycock ride beginning at the bridge:

> *On a haycock sleeping soundly*
> *The river rose and took me soundly*
> *Down the current; people cry'd*
> *'Sleeping!' down the stream I hy'd*
> *'Where away' quoth they 'from Greenland?'*
> *No, from Wansford Brigs in England.*

Born one summer night in 1488, in a cave in the picturesque North Yorkshire town of Knaresborough, Ursula Sotheil was the illegitimate child of a young girl. She married carpenter Toby Shipton and became known as Mother Shipton, a celebrated prophetess and England's equivalent to Nostradamus. All of her prophecies were passed on by word of mouth until 1641, when the first of some fifty versions were published. By this time many of them had already become true, but she also spoke of horseless carriages, ships made of iron, manned flight and predicted that "around the world thoughts shall fly, in the twinkling of an eye.". She is said to have predicted her own death in 1561, after which she was buried in unconsecrated ground outside the walls of York. The name of the sign is taken from her most famous prophecy: "The world to an end shall come, in eighteen hundred and eighty one."

The World's End, *Knaresborough*

The Pillars of Hercules, Greek Street, London W1

A brick and half-timbered pub, The World's End, at the corner of Waterside, displays her image, stylised as a medieval witch. An 1822 directory lists an earlier inn called the World's End on this site. Across the bridge is Mother Shipton's Cave and petrifying well around which everyday items are hung below the falling waters. It is claimed that a teddy bear can be turned to stone by the water's mineral deposits in only three months.

To the ancients, the world's end was literally its edge, at the western end of the Mediterranean, guarded by the Pillars of Hercules, in the form of the Rock of Gibraltar and Mount Hacho. The legend was that Hercules split the one rock into two in order to reach Cadiz. A popular London pub in Greek Street bears their name.

The only English city to be acclaimed a World Heritage Site for its Georgian architecture, Bath owes much of its fame to Richard Nash. Known as Beau Nash, he came to Bath in 1703, the year after Queen Anne's visit to the spa. He made his newly adopted home the centre of fashion and elegance after his self-appointment in 1734 as unofficial master of ceremonies. Among his duties were to vet visitors aspiring to be accepted into the city's society, find appropriate dancing partners for the ladies (virtually the role of society marriage-broker), and to regulate gambling. For much of his life he supported his dandy lifestyle from his own gambling, which eventually proved his downfall and he died a pauper. In spite of this, in recognition of his services to the city's eighteenth-century tourist industry he was buried in Bath Abbey.

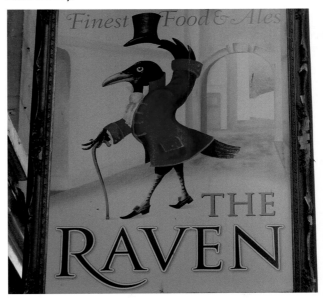

The Raven, Bath

On the corner of Quiet Street and the cobbled Queen Street stands a pub bearing the sign of The Raven. Originally the raven featured in the arms of Queen Mary I, but this one is the Beau Nash-esque man-about-town, seen walking along outside his namesake pub, with the picturesque archway in the background. The building dates from around 1780, some nineteen years after Nash's death, and in 1914 became Quiet Street Wine Vaults, then Hatchett's, before acquiring its present name, brought by the new landlord who had moved from another Bath pub.

Out of the Dark Ages

The Swordsman, Stamford Bridge

On 5 January 1066, Edward the Confessor, King of England and son of Æthelred the Unready and Emma of Normandy, died. He was buried in the abbey he had built at Westminster.

The pious Edward died without a son and heir, and Harold, son of the Saxon Earl Godwin, took the kingship. There were other claimants to the throne, from lands to the north and south, and soon an army of Norsemen led by Harald Hadrada landed on England's North Sea coast. Hadrada was accompanied by Harold's renegade brother Tostig, with a contingent of Flemish warriors. On 20 September at Fulford Gate outside York they faced a defending army led by Edwin of Mercia and Morcere of Northumbria, earls of the two former northern Saxon kingdoms. The Saxon earls were defeated along the waterlogged banks and marshes of the River Ouse.

On the same day, King Harold and his army set out to meet the invaders. He reached York five days later. The Norsemen, meanwhile, were encamped ten miles away, at Stamford Bridge along the banks of the Derwent, awaiting Saxon hostages. On the blisteringly hot day, many had left their armour on board their ships. Taken by surprise, they were soon driven off the west bank, but a Viking hero single-handedly held the wooden bridge while his comrades regrouped. It is said that a group of Saxons took a rowing boat and speared him to death from below.

Once the bridge was taken, the invaders were slaughtered by repeated charges interspersed with volleys from the Saxon archers. Between 240 and 500 longships had been used to carry the Norsemen across the sea. Only twenty-four were needed to carry the survivors home with the body of their leader.

The Viking challenge was over but news from the south took Harold and his men on a 250-mile march to Hastings to face a new enemy. There, on the morning of 14 October, the last invader, William the Conqueror, won the most famous battle fought on English soil. William was crowned in Westminster Abbey on Christmas Day.

The Battle of Hastings is commemorated on the Bayeux Tapestry. Between the words "*Hic Harold Rex Interfectus Est*" ("Here King Harold is killed") a red dragon standard is depicted. Beneath is a figure shot in the eye by a Norman archer, giving rise to the legend of how Harold died, although many historians now believe that the King is the figure next to him, cut down by a Norman cavalryman. The dragon was the standard of the West Saxons, although The Green Dragon is now a more common present-day English inn sign than the red one.

The Green Dragon, Lincoln. *The timber-framed Green Dragon on Lincoln's waterfront was once a medieval guest house belonging to St Catherine's Priory.*

William the Conqueror died twenty-one years after Hastings, leaving his Norman dukedom to his son Robert and the kingdom of England to his son William Rufus.

The village of Brough in Cumbria stands on the route of an old Roman road on the site of a fortification built as a defence against the Brigantes, an ancient British tribe. William II, called Rufus supposedly because of his red hair, built one of England's first castles here in 1090, but it was to survive less than a hundred years, destroyed by the Scottish King William the Lion in 1174. A few years later the present castle was built. Now in ruins, it is shown on the sign of the nearby Castle Hotel, a large black-and-white eighteenth-century coaching inn on the old London to Glasgow mail route.

William Rufus was one of England's least popular kings. He was born about ten years before the Norman invasion of 1066. Although politically successful in acquiring territory, he succeeded in alienating the Church, the barons and the common man. He gained control of his older brother Robert's lands in Normandy by financing Norman participation in the Crusades. Taxing Englishmen to raise the funds, he stayed at home feasting and hunting while the Normans travelled east.

The Castle Hotel, Brough

Rufus is said to have imposed strict laws in the royal hunting grounds of the New Forest; blinding, mutilation or death awaited anyone caught disturbing the king's deer. His reign came to an end on 2 August in the year 1100. On that morning, embarking on a hunt in the New Forest, he gave three arrows to Sir Walter Tyrell, the man regarded as the best archer in England. Later that day, his body was found beneath an oak tree, killed by one of those arrows.

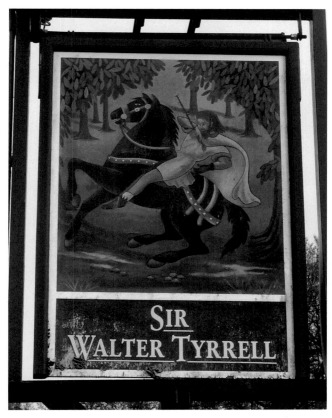

The Sir Walter Tyrell, Brook

The Stag in Lyndhurst, a small town in the New Forest

The official story was that a shot from Tyrell had rebounded off the tree, and by this time the knight was safely in France. William's younger brother Henry had hastened to Winchester, seized the royal treasury and proclaimed himself king. His coronation was held only three days later and the new king was not inclined to pursue the man to whom he owed his crown. By 1106 Henry was also ruler of Normandy. On 1 December

1135 he died at a hunting lodge near Rouen, the capital of his Norman duchy, after eating a dish of lampreys.

A pub called the Sir Walter Tyrell stands on the edge of the Hampshire village of Brook in the New Forest. Unusually, it does not show the man whose name it bears. Instead it shows the mortally wounded Rufus falling from his horse.

A-hunting We Will Go

Venison is now thought of as the meat of deer, but in *Pub Names of Britain*, Dunkling and Wright tell us that it once applied to the flesh of any animal killed in the chase, including boar and hare. The Haunch of Venison claims to be Salisbury's oldest inn. It was built in about 1320, of wattle and daub around a frame from ships' timbers, to house the medieval workers who were constructing the cathedral's spire. Salisbury Cathedral is England's tallest, standing at 404 feet. It seems that the inn was once owned by St Thomas's Church and licensed in the early sixteenth century, but in its early days it was said to have been used as a house of ill repute.

It is claimed that a ghostly white lady has been seen from the rear windows, which overlook the small graveyard of St Thomas's. Upstairs in the inn unexplained footsteps have been heard between 11.30 and midnight. There is the story of a cheating card player whose hand was chopped off by a butcher. Ghost hunters may say that the discovery of a mummified hand here in the nineteenth century is proof that the card player is still searching.

The Haunch of Venison, *Salisbury*

within his jurisdiction to the king. To avoid robbery the documents were hidden in a pie, but John removed one of them, the deeds to Mells, to keep for himself and his descendants. The abbot had refused to surrender the abbey and was imprisoned, tortured and eventually executed. The charge against him was robbery, as a charge of treason might have made Englishmen consider him a martyr. Ted Bruning tells us the story in his Historic Inns of England, *adding that the inn in the picturesque Somerset village of Mells has been owned by the Horner family since before Henry VIII's Reformation.*

The Salamander, *a busy bar in John Street, Bath, behind a shop-style frontage and listed in the* **Good Pub Guide**. *Its sign, of the creature reputed to be able to walk through fire, originates from the seared chops and steaks cooked here.*

> *Little Jack Horner sat in a corner,*
> *Eating a Christmas pie.*
> *He put in his thumb and pulled out a plumb,*
> *And said 'What a good boy am I!'*

The old nursery rhyme concerns the legendary John Horner, who was entrusted by his master the Abbot of Glastonbury to deliver the deeds of the twelve abbeys

The Talbot, *Mells*

The Horse & Hound, *Broadway, an inn built from golden Cotswold stone in the heart of a picturesque Worcestershire village*

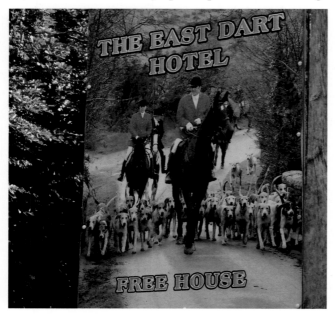

The East Dart Inn, *Postbridge*

It is practically unchanged since the time it was built. The wall behind the Tithe Barn Bar is painted with a large idyllic scene featuring farm workers and travellers, with a large plough hanging above. It bears the sign of the talbot, a hunting dog now extinct, which featured in the arms of the Talbot family, Earls of Shrewsbury.

Like a rocket shot to a ship ashore
The lean red bolt of his body tore
Like a ripple of wind running swift on grass
Like a shadow on wheat when a cloud blows past…

John Masefield's *Reynard the Fox* describes the eponymous hero's flight and escape from the huntsman and his hounds. In 2001 it was reported that more than two hundred thousand people took part in fox-hunting in Britain. In Norman England deer and boar had been hunted, but only by the Royal Family.

It was to be six hundred years later, during Charles II's reign, that hounds were first trained specifically to hunt foxes. One source claims that the first hunt, in the Yorkshire Dales, was founded by the Duke of Buckingham – he died in 1687 of a chill, caught while hunting.

The Mid-Devon Hunt claims to have first been held in 1604. It starts out from the village of Postbridge and runs along the River Dart and over the north-east of Dartmoor. Postbridge's The East Dart Inn depicts the hunt.

The Live & Let Live, *Downham Market*

British and North American fox-hunting differed in that the British aim was to kill the fox, protecting the farmer's livestock.

After campaigns against cruel sports and protests from traditionalists, in 2005 the hunting of foxes and other animals with dogs in England became illegal. However, hunt meetings without the kill are still held and the sound of hunting horns and spectacle of scarlet-coated riders still grace the English countryside. Inn signs recalling the hunting era are still seen throughout England, though not all of them celebrate the fox's fate.

On the edge of the small Norfolk town of Downham Market stands the Live and Let Live, with the sign of the huntsman and his quarry sharing a drink. An earlier sign here, in the 1960s, showed a cat looking benignly at chickens perched on its back.

The Snooty Fox in Tetbury takes the fox's liberty a step further; now it is the intelligent beast which looks with disdain at the subservient hounds. The Elizabethan coaching inn facing the Gloucestershire town's iconic centrepiece, its covered marketplace, was formerly the White Hart. It was renamed in 1979. Inside, a 'life-size' cuddly red-coated fox stands in the foyer.

Falconry, the hunting of live quarry with trained birds, spread across Asia to the Germanic tribes in the sixth century and for the next thousand years was popular in Britain and continental Europe. Some say the sport originated in China, others that a Persian king, impressed by watching a falcon in the wild, ordered it to be caught and trained to fly from the hand.

The Snooty Fox, Tetbury

The Falcon, Stratford-upon-Avon

Strictly speaking, falconers use long-winged hawks and hawkers, or austringers, use the shorter-winged birds.

Shakespeare's crest was a falcon holding a spear. A private house in Shakespeare's day, The Falcon in Stratford had become a public house by 1640. In 1823 the Shakespeare Club was founded here. Falconry was originally practised to provide food for the table, but by medieval times it had become a status symbol. Kings used the white gyr falcon, which today sell for a small fortune, and princes used the peregrine falcon shown on the Stratford inn's sign. Servants used the kestrel and there were punishments laid out for anyone who dared to fly a bird above his status. Falconry was popular among the clergy, and nuns were warned against bringing their hawks into church.

***The Falcon**, Uppingham*

Elizabeth I's badge was a falcon wearing a golden crown. The heraldic falcon is displayed above the door of The Falcon in the marketplace at Uppingham. Dating from the sixteenth century, it was once the Rutland town's main coaching inn on the London to Leeds mail route.

Elizabeth's father Henry VIII had the Royal Mews at Charing Cross built to house his falcons, and at one time it was traditional for the Duke of Athol and Lord Derby to present the gift of a falcon at coronations. Falconry declined in popularity with the introduction of the shotgun.

The Kite at Osney near Oxford shows the sign of another bird of prey, the red kite. Once an endangered species, the red kite was saved from extinction by a long protection programme and was reintroduced into England in the 1990s. It can be seen wild mainly in the Chilterns.

The pheasant-shooting season runs from 1 October to 1 February. Some sources say it was the Romans who introduced pheasants into England from Asia, others that it was the Normans in the eleventh century. It is now the most important game bird in Britain with a population of more than three million. In medieval times they were hunted with hawks, shot with arrows or trapped with nets. A 1604 law dictated that the penalty for unlawfully taking a bird should be a fine of twenty shillings or three months imprisonment. No common man could have afforded the fine.

The Kite, *Osney*

The Golden Pheasant, *Burford*

An inn of golden Cotswold stone in Burford shows the sign of The Golden Pheasant *chrysolephus pictus*. Sometimes known as the Chinese pheasant, from their country of origin, they are poor flyers and spend most of their life on the ground. The vividly coloured males would seem to be easy targets. Some now live in the wild but they are most often seen in zoological gardens and aviaries.

Born an Angler

The Compleat Angler, *Norwich*

As no man is born an artist, so no man is born an angler.
Izaak Walton

Angling is said to be England's biggest participant sport, and perhaps even bigger in Scotland and Ireland where many happy hours have been whiled away catching salmon and trout. The most famous early work on the sport was written in 1653 by Izaak Walton – he called it *The Compleat Angler or the contemplative man's recreation*. Walton was born in 1653, son of a Staffordshire innkeeper, and later moved to London where he married in 1626. By 1640 he had lost his wife and all seven children. Two children by his second marriage, a son and a daughter, reached adulthood. Walton himself admitted he knew little about fly-fishing and recommended worms, grasshoppers and frogs as bait, saying of the frog, "Use him as though you loved him, that is, harm him as little as you may possibly, that he may live the longer."

On the Norwich waterfront off Prince of Wales Road the Compleat Angler stands, a spacious pub with a riverside beer garden. A plaque outside tells its history, saying that it was once an old Victorian coaching inn and contemplating how boisterous it must have been during the Second World War when patronised by British and American servicemen. Inside it displays extracts from Walton's book.

A stone-built ivy-clad inn in Bamford, Derbyshire, The Angler's Rest displays a stone sign on the roof and a more traditional sign of a smart Edwardian gentleman displaying his day's catch.

The Angler's Rest, Bamford

The Three Fishes *sign in Shrewsbury's Fish Street shows a perch, pike and salmon*

A Fighter by his Trade

Read here the moral roundly writ
For him who into battle goes -
Each soul that hitting hard or hit,
Endureth gross or ghostly foes,
Prince, blown by many overthrows,
Half blind with shame, half choked with dirt
Man cannot tell but Allah knows
How much the other side was hurt!

Rudyard Kipling's *Boxing*, from his *Verses on Games*, describes the English fighting spirit in the face of adversity. Shopping in Oxford Street can also be thirsty work. Around the corner in Wells Street, an antique pub stands on the site of a bare-fisted boxing booth once run by James Figg, the first world heavyweight boxing champion. He held the title from 1719 to 1730. Over the years the premises became run down until bought by Sam Smiths brewery in 1989. It is characterised by its extraordinary stained-glass windows surrounding the downstairs bar, designed by Ann Sotheran, depicting British champions of various walks of life: the likes of explorer David Livingstone, Edward Whymper, conqueror of the Matterhorn, and Florence Nightingale, nursing heroine of the Crimean War.

The six 'champions' shown on the sign are Captain Matthew Webb, the first to swim across the English Channel and who died trying to swim across Niagara Falls; jockey Fred Archer; boxer Bob Fitzsimmons, a Cornishman who moved to New Zealand at the age of nine and won the world heavyweight championship by knocking out Gentleman Jim Corbett on 17 March 1897; cricketer W. G. Grace; nineteenth-century Scottish golfer Young Tom Morris; and seven-times Wimbledon champion William Renshaw.

The Champion*, Wells Street, London W1*

Born near Bristol in 1781, the quietly-spoken Tom Cribb moved to London at the age of fifteen and found work as a coal porter on the banks of the Thames at Wapping. After serving in the Royal Navy at the start of the Napoleonic Wars he became a prize fighter, winning his first bare-knuckle bout in the year of Trafalgar, 1805, over seventy-six rounds lasting two hours and twenty minutes. In those days a round ended when a fighter was knocked down, and he was given thirty seconds to come to his senses before fighting on.

At five feet ten inches and normally weighing in at fourteen stone, Tom became known as the Black Diamond, from his coal-carrying days. After his only defeat, over fifty-two rounds early in his career, he began to take his sport more seriously and is credited with being the first boxer to follow a training programme. In December 1811, at a Monday-night dinner in the Castle Tavern in London's Holborn, after his second victory against the fighter Molineux, he was presented with a silver cup worth eighty guineas, an amount equivalent to five years' wages for the average working man. He was eventually recognised as world champion, his last fight being attended by fifteen thousand spectators.

After retirement, Tom took over the King's Arms in St James, London, the Golden Lion in Southwark, and finally the Union Arms on the corner of Oxendon Street and Panton Street near Piccadilly, where he was landlord for nineteen years. A rhyme was written in 1824 after a visit to his house:

The Champion, I see, is still on the list,
His standard 'The Union Arms':
His customers still he will serve with his fist,
But without creating alarms.
Instead of a 'floorer' he tips them a glass,
Divested of joking or fib:
Then 'Lads of the Fancy' don't Tom's house pass,
But take a hand at the game of Cribb.

Tom's fighting days were over, and when the German dwarf whom he employed in the pub was assaulted by a customer, the action he took was of a legal nature. A celebrity for the rest of his life, he accepted an invitation to George IV's coronation in 1821 and attended dressed as a page.

Tom died in 1848 at the age of sixty-six. It was 112 years before his pub was renamed in his honour. Inside, its walls display old prints and photographs of famous fighters. It was nineteen years after Tom's death that Sir John Sholto Douglas, eighth Marquis of Queensbury, introduced new rules for boxing, with boxing gloves and rounds of three minutes followed by a minute's rest. The Queensbury Rules took some time to establish themselves and it was not until 1889 that the last bare-knuckle world heavyweight championship bout was fought.

The Tom Cribb, London SW1

acquired from the Marquis of Salisbury, Queen Victoria's favourite prime minister, in 1892. It goes on to say, "Prior to this the pub had been known as the Coach & Horses and then Ben Caunt's Head, and was famous for promoting prize fighting. A much friendlier and welcoming atmosphere is assured these days!"

Landlord Caunt, known as the Nottingham Giant, was a famous bare-knuckle fighter and it was under his management in the early nineteenth century that the premises became a boxing venue. It seems to have developed into a wine merchant's and then a gin palace.

Listed in Roger Protz's *Britain's 500 Best Pubs* and the *Good Pub Guide*, The Salisbury in St Martin's Lane has one of the most striking pub interiors of London, dating from 1898 and restored in 1963. The ornate interior has red and dark wood-panelled ceilings, plush red wall-seating and stools, ornate copper-topped tables, stone and wooden square pillars. Frosted glass patterned mirrors around the interior wall match the windows. Ancient Roman-style statuettes support orange-shaded wall-lights with matching hanging ceiling shades in red and yellow.

A plaque outside tells us that the lease was

The Salisbury, St Martin's Lane, London WC2

Lionheart

Burrowed into the sandstone beneath Nottingham Castle are some of the rooms of what is often claimed to be England's oldest inn. There was once a brewhouse here providing ale for the castle's many inhabitants. A sign outside gives the date as 1189 and the inn's strange name sheds light on its past. "Ye Olde Trip to Jerusalem" was an invitation to rest on the way to the Third Crusade.

In 1187 news reached England of a disaster at the Horns of Hattin, by the shores of the Sea of Galilee. On 4 July of that year the heavily outnumbered occupying Frankish forces had been defeated by the great Muslim leader Salah al-Din Jusuf, better known as Saladin. A Saracen soldier wrote, "When we saw how many were dead we could not believe there were any prisoners, and when we saw the prisoners we could not believe that there were any dead." About thirty thousand of the Christian army were killed and a similar number captured. Within three months the city of Jerusalem had fallen.

Ye Olde Trip to Jerusalem, *Nottingham*

Two years later an army of eight thousand men led by Richard I, later to be know as Coeur de Lion, the Lionheart, prepared to sail from England for the Holy Land. They eventually landed at Acre in 1191, and after fighting his way to the gates of Jerusalem, Richard secured a treaty to guarantee safe access for pilgrims to the Holy Land.

Richard is shown on the sign of the Coeur de Lion, the city of Bath's smallest pub. Once a beer shop, a brewery and a house of ill repute, it has been the Coeur de Lion since about 1880 and is thought to be the only pub in England to bear this name.

The Lionheart's adventures on his way home are well documented. In spite of his dislike of the English climate, his failure to learn its language or to produce an heir, and his costing the population a small fortune in ransom money, he remains one of England's best-loved kings.

Strangely, a much more popular name for English inns is the Saracen's Head. One of these is at Towcester (pronounced *toe-ster*). It was once the town's main coaching inn on the London to Liverpool mail route via Coventry and Lichfield. It dates from seventeenth-century Restoration times, standing at the old crossing of Watling Street and the Oxford-Northampton road.

The Coeur de Lion, *Bath*

The Saracen's Head, *Towcester*

Known as the Pomfret Arms between 1832 and 1867, it reverted to its original name when the Earl of Pomfret's family, who lived nearby, died out. The inn still has its old coaching arch, and has a light-fitting in one of the conference rooms, made from the wheel from a nearby church bell tower. Charles Dickens gives a long account of Sam Weller's stay here. The inn also features in *Tom Brown's Schooldays*, the 1857 novel by Thomas Hughes set in Rugby School and featuring the notorious bully Flashman.

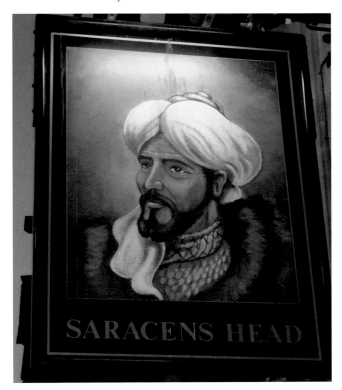

The Saracen's Head, Bath

Charles Dickens was reputed to have stayed at the Saracen's Head in Broad Street, Bath, in 1835 while working as a reporter covering Lord Russell's visit to the city. This ancient-looking inn was recorded in 1728.

The Turk's Head at the top of Bailgate in Lincoln, another version of the Saracen's Head name

One of England's most popular inn signs shows another theme from the Crusades, St George and the dragon. The legend tells of the medieval knight in

Libya, rescuing the princess and slaying the dragon, which represented Satan. The real St George seems to have been born in Turkey, a renowned Roman soldier whose parents were Christian. After protesting to the emperor Diocletian about the persecution of Christians he was imprisoned, tortured and beheaded in the Holy Land. In 1194 Richard the Lionheart adopted St George's cross, red on a white background, as England's national flag, and in the fourteenth century George replaced St Edmund as England's patron saint.

Among the many inns showing the slaying of the dragon is the George in Frome. It was the Somerset town's chief inn, servicing coaches on the mail route between Devizes and Wells, and as long ago as 1783 coaches called here travelling between the Belle Sauvage in London and the White Hart in Bath.

The George, Frome

Men in Lincoln Green

On his way home from the Crusades, Richard was shipwrecked and captured by Duke Leopold of Austria in 1192. He was imprisoned in the castle of Durnstein, high above the Danube, where he was held for ransom. The old ballad *A Gest of Robyn Hode* tells of events in England at the time. It begins:

> *Lythe and listin, gentilmen,*
> *That be of frebore blode;*
> *I shall you tel of a gode yeman*
> *His name was Robyn Hode*

While Richard was away and his brother John ruled, legend has it that Robin Hood and his Merry Men inhabited Sherwood Forest, robbing from the rich to feed the poor, and to help raise the King's ransom. Passed down in ballad and rhyme for more than 600 years, tales have been told of Robin, his sweetheart Maid Marian, the giant Little John, the minstrel Alan a Dale,

***The Green Man**, Malton*

Will Scarlet, Much the miller's son, the rotund Friar Tuck and the evil Sheriff of Nottingham. Robin, clad in Lincoln green, is displayed on the sign of The Green Man in Malton, an eighteenth-century market-day inn.

A pub sign in Churchgate, Retford, depicting a Robin Hood-like figure, bears the name The Sherwood Ranger. The unit was raised as the Nottinghamshire Yeomanry Cavalry in the summer of 1794, almost six hundred years after the legendary outlaw lived in Sherwood Forest

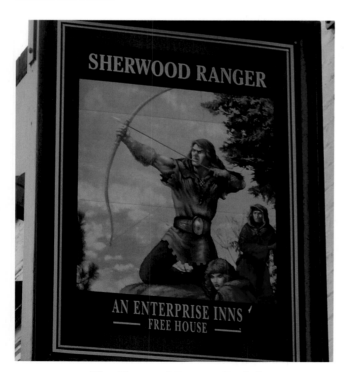

The Sherwood Ranger, *Retford*

It was another hundred years or more before it first saw active service, in the Boer War in 1900. Its men served as cavalry for most of the First World War, but as infantry in Gallipoli, and saw significant action in World War II in Africa. It was involved in the D-Day landings of June 1944, and the same year it became the first British unit to fight on German soil.

On the banks of the Seine stands the ancient town of Vernon, a staging post halfway between Paris and Rouen, with many old half-timbered buildings and a picturesque water mill. On the river's right bank there is a memorial stone inscribed in French and in English:

Nottinghamshire Sherwood Rangers Yeomanry Royal Armoured Corps.
In honoured remembrance of all our comrades and of the townsfolk of Vernon
who gave their lives in the battle for the liberation of this town August 1944.
They died that we might live.

Close by, the Rue Sainte Geneviève, running behind the town hall, is decorated with colourful hanging signs of fruit, flowers and food. One could be forgiven for thinking that Geneviève was the patron saint of inn signs.

One of the signs in Rue Sainte Geneviève in Vernon

Apples and Cheese

The Bramley Apple, *Southwell*

In Church Lane in the small Nottinghamshire town of Southwell stands a small pub and restaurant with a cottage-like appearance, named after Britain's most popular cooking apple.

A few doors away, at number 75, a light blue round plaque reads, "The Bramley Apple tree was grown from a pip by a young lady, Mary Anne Brailsford, between 1809 and 1815. It was thought that it came from an apple grown on a tree at the bottom of her garden (now No 75). One seedling produced a crop of very large apples in 1837 when the new occupier was Mr Matthew Bramley. A local gardener, Henry Merryweather, later obtained permission to take cuttings from the tree and it was duly registered the Bramley seedling."

Ye Olde Cheshire Cheese, London EC4

This modern world so stiff and pale
You leave behind you when you please
For long clay pipes and great old ale
And beefsteaks at the Cheshire Cheese

So the Scot John Davidson wrote of Ye Olde Cheshire Cheese in Fleet Street, the street where his poems were published in the 1890s. It seems to be listed in almost every guide to English inns. Enthusiastic patrons have included Charles Dickens and probably Dr Johnson, whose house nearby is now a museum. In *The Forsyte Saga* John Galsworthy mentions the great pies that were served here. They weighed up to 80 lbs and contained steak, kidneys, oysters, larks, mushrooms and spices.

In medieval times the site was occupied by a guest house of the Whitefriars, sold as an inn after the dissolution of the monasteries in 1538. It was rebuilt over its ancient cellar after the Great Fire of 1666 and named after the most popular English cheese of its time. The present-day customer will find its oak-panelled cubicles, small rooms, and narrow corridors as difficult to navigate as the buxom barmaids did in the days of table service.

Made from the full cream of cow's milk, one of England's oldest and most famous contributions to the world's blue cheeses is Stilton. On the basis of eighteenth-century documents, it was believed that Stilton cheese had originated in Melton Mowbray in Leicestershire, and laws were passed that the cheese could be manufactured only in Leicestershire, Derbyshire and Nottinghamshire. In September 2009 a recipe was discovered dated 1722 for a pressed cooked steamed cheese produced in the Cambridgeshire village of Stilton.

The attractive sign of **The Cheshire Cheese** *in Little Essex Street, London WC2, a simple and welcoming Victorian pub close to Victoria Embankment and Temple underground station*

It is to former landlord Cooper Thornhill that Stilton cheese owes its widespread fame, being sold to travellers on the great coaching journeys. Many would have taken cheeses home as souvenirs or gifts: no doubt its aroma was a welcome change from that of the unwashed, perspiring passengers, travelling huddled together in the sweltering, uncomfortable stagecoaches for days on end. The Bell declined with the coming of the railways but has returned to its former glory and is now as charming as it must have been in the days of the York Highflyer.

Ye Olde Cheshire Cheese, *a white pebble-dash half-timbered building in Castleton, Derbyshire. Its sign shows the cheese being enjoyed by customers from all walks of life.*

The golden-coloured Bell stands in the village, facing majestically across the wide and empty street that was once the Great North Road. It was built in the early seventeenth century with tall chimneys, mullioned windows and many gables and was one of the busiest inns of the coaching era.

The Bell, *Stilton*

To Market, to Market!

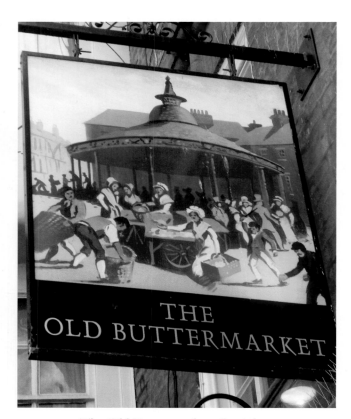

The Old Buttermarket, *Canterbury*

Surrounding the market squares in England's medieval cities and towns were many old inns, not just for refreshment, but to accommodate the many farmers and carters who travelled for hours from the countryside to ply their trade. The sign on the sixteenth-century inn called The Old Buttermarket, close to Canterbury Cathedral, shows the covered market that was here long ago. Musicians and street entertainers surround the war memorial that now stands in the square. Tunnels lead from the cathedral to the inn, possibly used by monks in days long gone by to enjoy a secret tipple while supposedly at prayer.

The Old Market Inn, overlooking Winchester Cathedral green

In the comparatively large cities there were marketplaces for each commodity. Wool and cloth, corn, hay, butter, fruit, fish, butcher meat, game and poultry were all sold in separate markets, not for the convenience of the customer but to enforce fair pricing and quality standards. In 1301 an ordinance in York restricted the hours for selling fish and prevented its resale, and penalised middlemen from buying any goods and selling them on at a profit. If they were caught, their goods would be confiscated.

The Market Inn, Salisbury

The Market Inn, Huntingdon

Many kinds of food were available in the old marketplace, but very few people would dine to the standards set by the medieval banquets recreated today. Little meat was available and the common man's diet lacked many vitamins. Most often his meal was pottage, a stew made from peas, beans and onions, with perhaps leeks, spinach and cabbage leaves thrown into the pot.

Potatoes had yet to be discovered in the New World. Rye was used for bread and barley for beer, but wheat from the miller was expensive. It became more easily available after the Black Death, when there were only half as many mouths left to feed.

Know as the City Tavern until 1865, the Market Tavern stands in Durham's Market Square. A plaque outside tells us that it was only in 1851 that an Act of Parliament allowed meat, fish and poultry to be sold here. Two years later the city fathers declared the water in the square to be unfit for human consumption. The delighted landlord of the Tavern must have seen a massive increase in his beer sales.

The Market Tavern, *Durham*

The Three Feathers

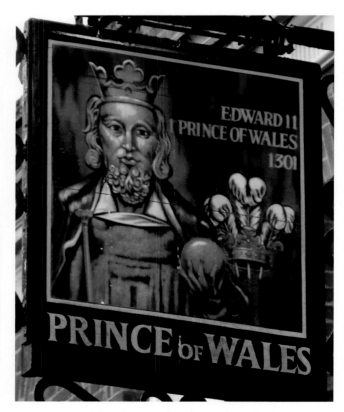

The Prince of Wales, *Falmouth*

Edward I had promised the Welsh a prince of their own, one who could not speak a word of English. An improbable story tells that he held up his baby son, who was too young to speak at all, and proclaimed him Prince of Wales. The young Prince Edward had been born at Caernarfon on 25 April 1284. At the age of sixteen he was given his princely title at a parliament in Lincoln. His portrait is shown on an inn sign in the Cornish town of Falmouth.

The Prince's father had been named Edward in honour of Edward the Confessor, Saxon King of England. With dark curly hair and a swarthy complexion and, at six feet two inches tall, head and shoulders above his subjects, he was nicknamed 'Longshanks'. Having fought in the Crusades as a young man, he set about the conquest of Wales to unite the two nations. In Scotland, he defeated William Wallace at Falkirk in 1298, recreated in the spectacular but historically wildly inaccurate film *Braveheart*. Edward I died at the age of sixty-eight and was buried in robes of red and gold, wearing a guilt crown in Westminster Abbey under a stone slab inscribed "Edwardus primus scotorum maleus". (Edward, I, the Hammer of the Scots.)

Edward II found his father a hard act to follow. The unpopular King was forced to abdicate in 1327 in favour of his fourteen-year-old son, who became Edward III. The forty-two-year-old ex-king was taken to Berkeley Castle virtually under house arrest and prevented from communicating with potential supporters. Some months later it was reported that he had died of a broken heart. Conspiracy theories still abound. Perhaps he was murdered; perhaps he escaped and lived in Italy as a monk. His supposed body, wrapped in a shroud perhaps to hide its true identity, was taken to various public places for mourning before burial.

His tomb and effigy can be found in Gloucester Cathedral and became an attraction for pilgrims throughout England.

The galleried chestnut-timbered New Inn in Gloucester was built in 1457 for pilgrims visiting the shrine. From the main street the frontage looks plain but an inn sign gives a clue to what lies behind: one of the most beautifully preserved coaching yards in the world, full of old-world charm, with benches and tables, flower baskets, barrels, overhead creepers and galleries on all four sides. Some five and a half centuries old, it still keeps its original name.

***The New Inn**, Gloucester*

An old coaching inn going by the sign of the Black Lion stands in Little Walsingham, on the former mail route from Norwich to Cromer. In 1061 an appearance of the Virgin Mary was reported in this Norfolk village and it soon became one of the world's most important pilgrimage sites. The inn stands in

Friday Market Place, next to the Church of the Assumption, consecrated in 2007, but the inn has been here much longer, having been offered for sale with eight acres of meadow and pasture ground in 1781.

The Black Lion, *Little Walsingham*

The sign of the Black Lion is taken from the arms of Queen Philippa of Hainault. She came from what is now Belgium and married the future King Edward III in York Minster on 24 January 1328 at the tender age of fifteen. Two years later they were crowned King and Queen. Philippa bore Edward fourteen children, though not all survived childhood. Their eight sons included John of Gaunt and Edward, the Black Prince. Queen Philippa is perhaps most famous for her plea to Edward for the lives of the Burghers of Calais in 1347 during the Hundred Years War. One of the twelve casts of Auguste Rodin's magnificent sculpture is displayed in Victoria Tower Gardens in London.

The King's Head, *Santa Monica, California*

The portrait of Edward III appears on a 'British Pub' sign almost 5,500 miles from England, in Santa Monica, California. The King was destined to rule England for fifty years, and it was his ambition to rebuild the age of chivalry and recreate a select order of knights modelled on King Arthur's legendary round table. It is said that the opportunity presented itself at a ball in Calais in 1348. In those days it was customary for young men to wear their sweetheart's garter either in their hat or around their knee as a token of their affection. As Joan, Countess of Salisbury, danced at the ball her garter fell to the floor. The King picked it up and, seeing his courtiers' disapproving glances, he tied the blue riband around his own knee saying, "*Honi soit qui mal y pense*" ("Shame on him who thinks ill of it").

Edward founded the Order of the Garter, still today England's noblest Order of Chivalry, restricted to twenty-four Knights Companions and a handful of officials and foreign royals. Its sign hangs outside a 200-year-old inn in London's Poland Street, displaying the French motto on the blue band.

Edward's reign saw two events which affected England for generations to come. The first was the start of the Hundred Years War with France. It began well for Edward, with a victory near Sluys off the Dutch coast giving him control of the seas, followed by the famous victory on land at Crécy. Then came the second momentous event. Between 1348 and 1350 the Black Death swept across England. The first wave took between a third and a half of the population and subsequent epidemics continued for the next 300 years, ending in the Derbyshire village of Eyam, whose small population courageously sealed itself off from the outside world until the danger of contagion had passed and most of them had succumbed.

***The Star & Garter**, London W1*

In 1369 at Windsor Castle, it took the life of Queen Philippa, who was much mourned throughout England. Her beautifully sculptured tomb now graces Westminster Abbey.

The Three Feathers

The plague seriously weakened England's ability to field an invading army, and in spite of an overwhelming victory at Poitiers on 19 September 1356 it would be almost sixty years before another famous battle could be celebrated by an English king.

On 26 August 1346 the blind King John of Bohemia was killed at the battle of Crécy. Fighting against him was Edward, Prince of Wales, known as the Black Prince from the colour of his armour. It was said that he had a great respect for the King and took the King's helmet, arrayed with ostrich feathers, from the battlefield to adopt as his badge. The German motto *"Ich Dien"* ("I serve") was also King John's. Prince Edward died at the age of forty-five, destined never to become King. His son became Richard II.

His badge is a popular inn sign throughout England. The seventeenth-century Plume of Feathers in the Square at Portscatho stands a few yards from the beach of a picturesque Cornish fishing village. It has two signs, one a fishing boat and the other the ostrich plume.

The Plume of Feathers, *Portscatho*

Some pride of place must be given to a famous old inn in Ludlow, with a spectacular timbered frontage. The Feathers was described in 1983 in the *New York Times* by historian Jan Morris as, "The most handsome inn in the world… one of the prime images of Olde England portrayed wherever tourism is known."

Well-deserved praise for this spectacular building with its beautiful timbered façade built in 1619, with faded wooden beams, balconies and carved heads. During the English Civil War, The Feathers was used to billet Royalist troops. They must have been disappointed that it did not become an inn until 1670, but no doubt they were well watered and fed. The inn was once home to prizefighting, cockfighting and the less bloody game of billiards.

the investiture of Charles Stuart as Prince of Wales in 1616. He was crowned Charles I nine years later. Its timbered frontage from roof to floor is not quite as impressive, but its interior is more so. Standing proudly in the High Street, it is a varied collection of English style. The Elizabethan house has a top storey added in Jacobean times and a rear wing built in Cromwell's time. An old manor house became part of the inn during the Georgian period. Mail coaches were still calling here in 1876.

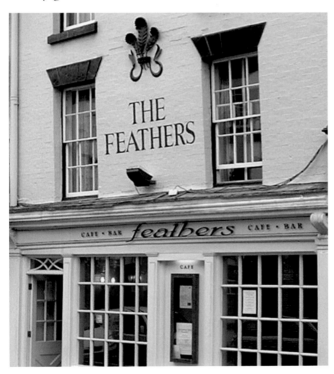

The Feathers, Ludlow

The half-timbered The Feathers in Ledbury, Herefordshire must be a close rival to its namesake in Ludlow. It seems to have been named to commemorate

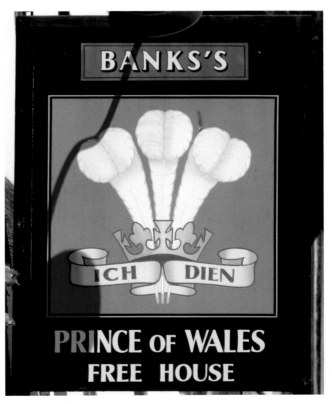

The Feathers, Ledbury

The Red Lion

In 1864, seventy-three inns called the Red Lion were recorded in London alone. Most authorities seem to agree that the Red Lion is England's favourite inn name, followed by the Royal Oak, the Cross Keys and the Crown.

The Inn Sign Society says that the sign of The Red Lion became more popular as the Lion of Scotland when James I took the English throne in 1603. The King, who was also James VI of Scotland, ordered that all important London buildings should display the Red Lion. Originally it signified the badge of John of Gaunt. Younger brother of Edward, the Black Prince, he was Edward III's fourth son, born in 1340 in Ghent. The Flemish city was called Gaunt in English. By his first marriage, to his cousin Blanche, John became Duke of Lancaster.

The Red Lion, *enjoying his beer on the corner of Dear Street in Market Rasen, Lincolnshire*

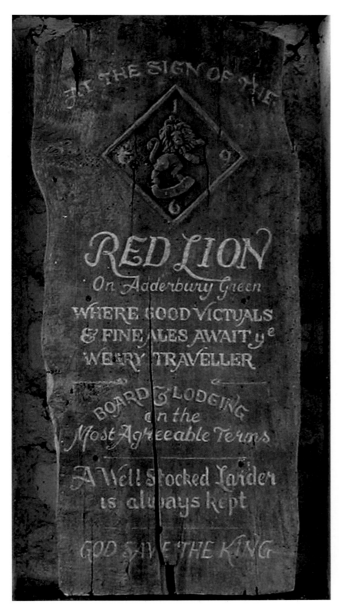

A Red Lion overlooks the village green in Adderbury, Oxfordshire. It was a coaching inn on the London to Stourport mail route and was known at one time as the Travellers Inn. It dates back to Tudor times and restoration work has uncovered coats of arms of Henry VIII and of the local Bustard family in one of the bedrooms. Before the Civil War it was a Royalist-owned inn and became a hiding place for many fleeing soldiers, some of whom dug an escape tunnel here. A list of landlords since 1690 is displayed in the bar.

The Red Lion, *Adderbury*

The Red Lion *in Bramham, West Yorkshire*

The Red Lion

The Red Lion

The Red Lion *in Parliament Street, London SW1. There has been a pub on this site since 1437, but the present one dates from 1845. In Charles Dickens'* **David Copperfield**, *the eponymous hero asks here for "a glass of Genuine Stunning ale".*

John of Gaunt's second marriage was to Constance, daughter of Pedro the Cruel of Castile. For sixteen years he schemed and fought for the throne of Castille and Leon but eventually gave up his claim in favour of his daughter. While he was fighting on the Scottish border, the Peasants' Revolt broke out and his Savoy Palace in London was burnt down.

John's nephew Richard II had become King in 1377 but the relationship gradually deteriorated. John was becoming unpopular, partly because of his military disappointments, and he was accused of conspiracy against the crown. Soon after his son Henry was exiled John died, on 3 February 1399. He was buried in the old St Paul's Cathedral near the high altar.

Richard II had become King at the age of ten. Within four years he had a rebellion on his hands. A generation before, the Black Death had made its grim appearance in England and by the 1370s had halved England's workforce, which was composed mainly of serfs, tied to the land and virtually owned by the nobility. The King and his followers had to make the most out of their reduced human resources, particularly with the Hundred Years War to pay for. Imposition of poll tax for the third year out of four led to civil unrest throughout the land. The tax was imposed per head at the same rate for rich and poor alike. In the spring of 1381 a rabble of some sixty thousand farm workers and town tradesmen converged on London from Kent and Essex in the Peasants' Revolt. Led by forty-year-old Wat Tyler, the force in Kent sacked Canterbury before meeting their Essex neighbours on Blackheath. Taking control of the city of London, they beheaded Treasurer Robert Hales and Archbishop of Canterbury Simon Sudbury on Tower Hill.

At Smithfield on 15 June 1381, the anniversary of the signing of the Magna Carta 166 years before, Englishmen once more sought their freedom. With twenty thousand men behind him Wat Tyler rode out alone to meet the King. Among the King's companions was Sir William Walworth, Lord Mayor of London. Offended by Tyler's arrogance, Sir William took out his dagger and thrust it into the peasant leader's body. It is said that Tyler was taken by his supporters to St Bartholomew's Hospital, but was dragged out by the King's men and beheaded.

The teenage King had promised Tyler the abolition of serfdom and a pardon for all of the rebels, but retribution was swift and violent.

The memory of the Lord Mayor's deed lives on. Beneath his statue in Fishmongers Hall are the words:

Brave Walworth, Knight, Lord Mayor that slew
Rebellious Tyler in his alarmes.
The King did give him in lieu
The Dagger and the Cytyes armes

The Pride of Paddington, London W2

The dagger that murdered Tyler is now incorporated in the city of London's arms, replacing the sword, symbol of the martyrdom of St Paul, London's patron saint. The arms are shown on many of London's signs, including the inn sign of The Pride of Paddington, which stands on the corner of London's Craven Road.

After putting the revolting peasants firmly in their place, Richard then succeeded in alienating many of England's nobility, appointing unpopular ministers and demanding money to fight in France. The series of quarrels culminated in 1399 in the King's confiscation of John of Gaunt's lands. While Richard was at war in Ireland, John of Gaunt's heir Henry Bolingbroke rallied the King's enemies. Facing a much tougher proposition than the common rabble, Richard surrendered his crown and in 1400 died a horrible death in Pontefract Castle, its name taken from the Latin for "broken bridge". Meanwhile Bolingbroke had been crowned Henry IV.

The Pontefract Castle, London W1

An inn bearing the sign of The Pontefract Castle stands in Wigmore Street, just to the north of London's Oxford Street.

Once More Unto the Breach!

The Old Kings Arms, built of Cotswold stone and half–timbers in the Gloucester town of Chipping Campden, displays the royal arms used between 1405 and 1603. Chipping, in the town's name, means market.

The King's Arms in the Nottinghamshire village of Clarborough shows the king in full armour. Most likely the king is Henry V, hero of Shakespearian stage and of Agincourt. At the age of twenty-eight Henry was trapped in France with a small army of sick and exhausted men, fighting to recover Normandy from where his ancestors had invaded England almost 350 years before. Pursued by an army of fresh soldiers three times the size of his own force, his only choice was to stand and fight.

The Old Kings Arms, *Chipping Campden*

The King's Arms, *Clarborough*

The muddy killing fields of France were between the villages of Tramecourt and Agincourt. On St Crispin's Day, 25 October 1415, Henry's men-at-arms and longbowmen faced the pride of French chivalry. Bowmen made up four-fifths of Henry's army. In England use of the longbow was practised from childhood and the accomplished and muscle-trained rapid-firing archer could match the crossbowman's bolt with six of his own arrows.

Eager to be first to the kill, or to capture English nobles for ransom, the impatient French cavalry trampled their own crossbowmen as they charged into the narrowing gap between the woods that bordered the battlefield. The English arrows took their toll, darkening the autumn sky. Some historians believe that the main battle lasted only half an hour. The French heralds counted ten thousand of their dead, of whom they said only 1,600 were "of low birth". The chroniclers estimated English losses at between twenty-five and a hundred men. Shakespeare's Henry V proclaims:

> *Then shall our names, familiar in their mouths as household words*
> *Harry the King, Bedford and Exeter,*
> *Warwick and Talbot, Salisbury and Gloucester,*
> *Be in their flowing cups freshly remembered.*
> *This story shall the good man teach his son.*
> *And Crispin Crispian shall ne'er go by*
> *From this day to the ending of the world*
> *But we in it shall be remembered.*

Henry married Katherine of Valois, daughter of King Charles VII of France: if everything went as planned, the two kingdoms would produce a common heir. In 1422 their son, at the tender age of eight months, became King Henry VI of England. At a little over a year old, his grandfather died and for a time he also became King of France.

The Bear & Staff, *London WC2*

From the age of seven his tutor was Richard Neville, Earl of Warwick, the virtual ruler of England. In Shakespeare's Henry VI, Warwick describes his heraldic emblem:

> *My father's badge, old Neville's crest,*
> *the rampant bear chained to the ragged staff.*

Legend has it that the first earl killed a bear and the second killed a giant with his staff. Warwick's sign can be seen outside The Bear & Staff in Charing Cross Road, London, which was formerly known as the Bear and Ragged Staff.

By 1453 the Hundred Years War between England and France was over. In France only Calais was left in English hands.

Neither Up nor Down

The Blue Boar, *Chipping Norton*

In 1454 Henry VI suffered a bout of madness. Richard, Duke of York took over as protector, but on the King's recovery the following year he refused to hand back the kingdom, believing he had a better claim to the throne. The rival factions met at what has been called the first battle of St Albans on 22 May 1455. It was more akin to a street brawl. The three thousand Yorkists entered the unwalled city over ditches hastily dug by the two thousand defenders. Casualties numbered little more than a hundred when three of the King's leaders were killed and it was all over. Although Henry remained King, Richard remained in control.

The so-called Wars of the Roses, between the white rose of York and the red rose of Lancaster, had begun.

Richard's personal badge was the Blue Boar. Perhaps it was adopted as a corruption of Ebor, the shortened version of the Roman name for York. The emblem, also a device of the Earl of Oxford, is displayed on The Blue Boar in Chipping Norton, Oxfordshire, a rambling old coaching inn on the London to Ludlow mail route, its licence dating back to 1683.

On 30 December 1460 Richard, with about twelve thousand men, faced the Lancastrians. He had taken an uphill defensive position at Sandal Castle, but seeing only the Lancastrian centre he decided not to wait for reinforcements and moved downhill to attack. Caught by the thorny flanks of the red rose, he was killed and his army cut to pieces. The event is commemorated in an old nursery rhyme:

> *The Grand Old Duke of York,*
> *He had ten thousand men,*
> *He marched them up to the top of the hill,*
> *And he marched them down again.*
> *And when they were up they were up,*
> *And when they were down they were down,*
> *And when they were only half way up*
> *They were neither up nor down.*

After a series of Yorkist victories, the King was deposed and the Duke's eighteen-year-old son became Edward IV. Fought on Palm Sunday 1461, Towton in North Yorkshire was England's bloodiest battle with a hundred thousand men intent on hacking each other to death. Twenty-eight thousand were slaughtered to decide

who should rule England. Weapons and skeletons are still being found in the earth and the peal of the three commemorative bells cast a few years later for the nearby church in Saxton can still be heard over the battlefield.

Edward's reign is now regarded by many historians as the ending of the Middle Ages and the beginning of the Renaissance in England. His badge was the white lion, shown outside the pub of the same name in London's Covent Garden.

The White Lion, *London WC2*

Edward died of pneumonia on 9 April 1483 and was succeeded by his twelve-year-old son, who became Edward V. The young King's reign lasted only seventy-eight days before he and his brother were escorted to the Tower of London. The fate of the Princes in the Tower is still unknown, but their supposed murder is attributed to the Grand Old Duke of York's only surviving son, who became King Richard III.

Now is the winter of our discontent
Made glorious summer by this son of York

***The Gloucester Arms**, a black-and-white inn in Penrith, Cumbria, where Richard stayed in 1471 before he was King. The royal arms are supported by two white boars.*

These first lines of Shakespeare's play *King Richard III* are spoken by his much-maligned character Richard, then Duke of Gloucester. It is only at the end of Act III that Richard becomes King. The reference is to one of Richard's badges, the sun in splendour. His others were the white boar and, of course, the white rose.

Of these, until 1485, the White Boar was probably the most common as an inn sign. In that year the King fought at Bosworth Field in Leicestershire. The relatively small battle, with Richard's forces probably just short of eight thousand facing about five thousand of the enemy, was decided by treachery. The King, wearing a specially made crown around his helmet, embarked on England's last great charge of mounted knights in armour. It failed only because a group of his own men, with axes to grind and swords to wield, made a counter charge against him and changed the course of English history.

Richard became the last English king to die in battle, and was buried in the abbey of Grey Friars in Leicester. His last Shakespearian words "A horse, a horse, my kingdom for a horse" are cried as the Bard wrongly portrays him in the cowardly act of fleeing the battlefield. The Wars of the Roses were virtually over and the signs of the White Boar were repainted blue.

The victorious Henry pre-dated his kingship to the day before the battle and declared every man who had fought against him a traitor to his king and country. One hundred and twelve years later, the Tudor descendants of Henry VII were entertained by Shakespeare's staged version of the events.

The King's Head, *in Malton's marketplace, a double-fronted creeper-clad inn dating from the early nineteenth century or earlier and bearing the portrait of Richard III*

Born in 1789, Edmund Kean was regarded as the best Shakespearian actor of his day. He is commemorated by a Nottingham pub called the Kean's Head. He made his debut on the London stage in 1814 as Shylock. His abilities attracted the attention of King George III who commanded him to recite at Windsor.

The Kean's Head, *Nottingham*

Kean travelled to New York to play the part of Richard III and after his performance in Quebec the Huron Indian tribe made him their chief. By 1833 his marriage had broken down and his health was deteriorating. His last performance, as Othello, was at Covent Garden on 25 March that year, and within two months he had died. The Nottingham pub's sign shows him playing the part of Hamlet speaking to the skull of Yorick, the court jester.

Bishop and King

The Crown Inn at Bolton Percy, North Yorkshire

The Crown and the Cross Keys are among the top four favourite signs for English inns. There seem to be about five hundred Crown signs, and with all of its variations, the Old Crown, the Rose & Crown and so on, it probably takes first place. Its meaning is usually an expression of loyalty to the king, and sometimes an inn built on land owned by him. Needless to say, there was a time in the mid-seventeenth century when the sign virtually disappeared from the inns, but probably not from the hearts of many landlords. Cromwellian temperance was bad for business. The name of the Crown is said to have been first recorded in England in 1476 when a publican named Walter Walters was executed for joking that he would make his son "heir to the Crown".

The Crown, in Frome, Somerset, a seventeenth-century grade II listed building. It stood empty for twelve years until receiving a Heritage grant in 2004.

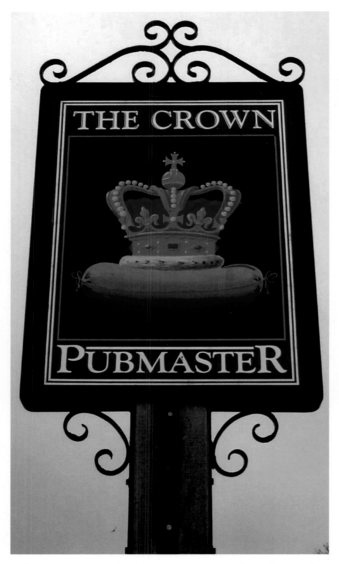

The Crown on the village green Hutton le Hole, North Yorkshire. The inn dates from the 1820s if not earlier and features timbered ceilings and log fires in stone fireplaces.

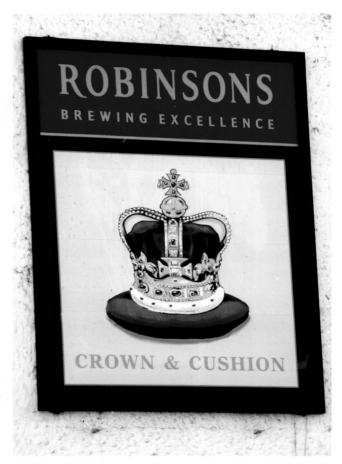

The Crown & Cushion in Appleby, Cumbria. The cushion is used to carry the crown to the new monarch at coronations.

The Cross Keys was the symbol of the Vatican, representing St Peter's keys to the Kingdom of Heaven. The inn sign would normally show that the inn was built on church lands. When the English crown opposed papal authority the sign survived, probably because many English churches remained dedicated to the first Pope, St Peter, and the arms of some bishops still displayed his symbol.

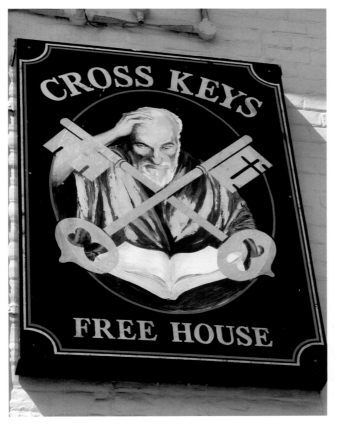

The Cross Keys on Old Dover Road, Canterbury

The Cross Keys, Chester

Bishop and King

The Cross Keys *in Thirsk, North Yorkshire. The inn dates from about 1830,*
but part of the building goes back to monastic times

The Cross Keys, *Stratford-upon-Avon*

The Ostrich, *Colnbrook*

Once known as the Hospice, the ancient Berkshire inn now bearing the sign of the Ostrich was built as a monastic guest house in 1108. It probably became an inn in the second half of the twelfth century and claims to be England's third-oldest inn. In the dim and distant past the name was corrupted and it now bears the sign of the fastest flightless bird.

The outside and interior echo its early life, with a wealth of antique memorabilia in the downstairs bar, and upstairs the Elizabethan and Jacobean rooms still evoke the age of the Tudors and Stuarts. Distinguished guests availing themselves of its hospitality have included King John on his way to sign the Magna Carta at Runnymede.

In the seventeenth century landlord Jarman and his wife had a bed attached to a trapdoor which dropped sleeping guests into a vat of boiling beer in the kitchen below. They are said to have robbed and disposed of sixty wealthy customers before they were hanged for their crimes.

The Busby Stoop, *Sandhutton*

An old inn called the Busby Stoop, near the village of Sandhutton in North Yorkshire, displays the intriguing sign of a cursed chair. The word 'stoop' is old northern English for a pillar or post. It was here that in 1702 landlord Thomas Busby was arrested for the murder of his father-in-law with a hammer. When dragged from his chair it was perhaps due to his intoxication that he cursed the chair and not those who took him to be tried and hanged outside his inn. His body was placed in a gibbet at the roadside to rot. His ghost, still with the noose around its neck, is said to haunt the inn, but his curse on the chair, that those who sit in it will meet a quick and violent end, is more disturbing.

Among those who have risked his malediction have been a World War II airman who was killed the following day, a motorcyclist killed on his way home from the inn, a hitch-hiker killed two days later and a customer who suffered a fatal heart attack the following night. In 1978 the landlord had the chair removed to a museum in Thirsk where it hangs high, well out of the reach of anyone wishing to tempt fate.

The London street of Crutched Friars, near Fenchurch Street Station, takes its name from the Augustinian order from Italy who settled here in about 1249. The friars had more than two hundred monasteries in Italy, and later founded other English settlements including those in York and Oxford. The friars were mendicants, owning nothing and living off charitable donations.

They were named from the Latin *Fratres Cruciferi*, literally "crossed brothers", as they carried a staff surmounted by a cross and their habit, first of black or brown and later blue, bore a red cross. The Crutched Friar pub here now bears a sign in their memory.

Many old inn signs were of biblical origin, back in days when religion was an integral part of the Englishman's everyday life and when the established church owned much of the land on which the inns were built. Ye Olde Salutation Inn in Nottingham, a small whitewashed single-fronted pub, displays the date 1240.

The Crutched Friar, *London EC3*

Ye Old Salutation, *Nottingham*

St Mary's Vaults *in Stamford, a small double-fronted pub in St Mary's Street, in a picturesque Lincolnshire town. The medieval spired church of St Mary is close by.*

The name is from St Luke's gospel where the angel appears to Mary in Nazareth to announce the birth of Christ. A plaque outside tells us "The present house was built c.1240 on the site of the 13th century ale house known as 'Archangel Gabriel Salute the Virgin Mary'". During the first Civil War 1642-46 part of the house was used, on separate occasions, as recruiting rooms for both factions.

The sign of The Hope and Anchor at Ross-on-Wye is also a biblical reminder, although some think the name is a corruption of the Hope Anchor, a ship's spare anchor for use in emergencies. The anchor is the New Testament symbol of Hope, mentioned in the anonymous epistle to the Hebrews. In the Old Testament's Book of Genesis it has the same meaning, the sign of God's covenant with Noah after

The Hope & Anchor, Ross-on-Wye

The Angel, Witney

the flood. It is known as the Noachide Covenant in Jewish and Christian religion, a precursor to the Ten Commandments, setting out a system of justice and prohibiting idolatry, blasphemy, murder, adultery, robbery and eating the flesh torn from a living animal.

The Angel stands in the market town of Witney in Oxfordshire in the market square facing the village green. In the seventeenth century the inn was known as the Greyhound. The town, on the edge of the Cotswolds, was once famous for its blanket making.

The Angel, Wetherby

The Angel in Wetherby was the town's main coaching inn between 1760 and 1840, claiming to be the halfway house between London and Edinburgh, although it was the London to Glasgow mail that called here each day while the Edinburgh mail took a more easterly route. With its own smithy, the Angel kept forty posting horses here for coaches to change, and had stabling for more than a hundred. After the coaching era the stables became a printing works but the old inn is still very much alive.

On the sign of the Angel & Crown in London's St Martin's Lane the Angel holds an inscription from Psalm 91: "He shall give His angels charge over thee to keep thee in all thy ways". A plaque outside tells us that Angel & Crown was a very popular name in the seventeenth century, especially after the restoration of Charles II to the throne in 1660. It goes on to say that that public house has stood here, in the centre of theatreland, since 1727. The area acquired a reputation for being one of the most notorious districts in London, where brothels flourished. It says: "Despite its disreputable character some notable people were connected to the area. The cabinet-maker Thomas Chippendale lived here, William Hogarth re-founded an art school that was attended by Thomas Gainsborough, Reynolds and Benjamin West, and the young Mozart lived in St Martin's Lane with his mother while touring Europe as a child prodigy.."

Oranges and lemons, say the bells of St Clement's.
You owe me five farthings, say the bells of St Martin's.
When will you pay me, say the bells of Old Bailey.
When I grow rich, say the bells of Shoreditch.
When will that be, say the bells of Stepney.
I do not know, says the great bell of Bow.

The old rhyme echoes the sound of the London bell chimes; a longer version calls out all fifteen of London's main parishes, each with its own local trades. *Oranges and Lemons*, a square dance recorded in the Great Plague year of 1665, was for the nearby wharves where citrus fruits were unloaded: St Martin's parish was home to the moneylenders.

It has been said that the bell speaks all languages. In England it has always been a popular inn sign and one of the oldest. Barrie Cox, in his 1994 *English Inn and Tavern Names*, traces one recorded back in 1403. The sign often refers to a church belfry nearby.

The church bell rang out the life of Englishmen in towns and villages, in celebrations and disasters. During the Second World War, the bells fell silent for six years, ready to signal the alarm should England's soil be invaded. The bell has summoned those in holy orders to their daily services and the common man to religious festivals, baptisms, marriages and funerals, his whole life from the cradle to the grave. Thomas Hood wrote in *Faithless Sally Brown*:

The Angel & Crown, *London WC2*

His death, which happened in his berth
At forty-odd befell
They went and told the sexton
And the sexton toll'd the bell.

The Bell in Nottingham's Angel Row claims to be the city's oldest inn, even older than the Trip to Jerusalem. Its cellars are said to date from Anglo-Saxon times. A smaller inn sign bears the date 1437. It is believed to have once been part of a Carmelite friary.

The Bell, Nottingham

The Bell, Welford on Avon

The Bell in Welford-on-Avon displays a real bell as its sign. The rambling old seventeenth-century coaching inn, in a small Warwickshire village with thatched cottages, regularly features in the *Good Pub Guide*.

The Bell *in Leominster, Herefordshire*

The Bell in Moretonhampstead, Devon, a black-and-white timbered pub in an ancient market town on the edge of Dartmoor

The Bell & Crown, London W4

The Bell & Crown is a riverside pub on the north bank of the Thames east of Kew Bridge in Strand on the Green, Hounslow. It now serves an affluent area of London, but when it was licensed in 1751 the clientele was very different. It was the haunt of smugglers who braved the treacherous muddy riverbank to bring their contraband ashore. Its name comes from the nearby church bells inscribed "Praise God. Honour the King".

Ye Olde Mitre stands close to Hatton Gardens, the heart of London's gold and jewellery trade. Said to date from 1546, the pub is hidden down Ely Court, off Ely Place, and its site was part of a garden in the Bishop of Ely's palace, perhaps his servants' quarters.

Ye Olde Mitre, London EC1

The Church Mouse in Chester le Street, County Durham

The wall outside displays a stone mitre with the date 1546. In the late sixteenth century Queen Elizabeth took some of the site from him, for a house to be built for her chancellor Sir Christopher Hatton. It is said that a cherry tree trunk in the corner of the front bar was the boundary between the bishop's land and the chancellor's.

Between two parishes, it was a haven for the local criminal community who had two escape routes from the parish constables. These days its clientele are more respectable businessmen, calling in for refreshments on their way home from the office.

The Mitre in Oxford was formerly a coaching inn. Its interior contains old beams and panels and a vaulted cellar dating from the thirteenth century. It is said that an underground passage leads under the High Street to the Chequers opposite.

The Mitre, Oxford

Close to Canterbury Cathedral, in Best Lane, is the Thomas Becket, a pub with old wooden floors and tables and a charming interior resembling an indoor vineyard.

The Thomas Becket, *Canterbury*

Born in London in 1118, and educated in England, France and Italy, Becket became Henry II's Chancellor and close friend, and in 1162 was appointed Archbishop of Canterbury. Henry's confidence that the statesman would bring the Church closer to being controlled by the crown was soon shattered by the Archbishop's shift in allegiance, and complex politics led to Thomas being forced to flee to France. Because of support for the exiled Archbishop from the Pope and King Louis VII of France, Henry was forced to recall him. Still in Normandy himself, the King's angry words "Will no-one rid me of this turbulent priest!" led to four knights crossing the channel and, on 29 December 1170, murdering the Archbishop in his cathedral. To restore credibility with his subjects, the penitent King long sought absolution from the Pope and on 12 July 1174 allowed himself to be flogged by the monks of Canterbury Cathedral as a final gesture. By this time the Church had already made the Archbishop a saint.

And specially from every shire's end
Of England they to Canterbury wend,
The holy blessed martyr there to seek
Who helped them when they lay so ill and weak

A shrine was built on the site of the assassination, and the way was marked by signposts, which became known as 'bishop's fingers'. It soon drew pilgrims from throughout England, immortalised in Geoffrey Chaucer's *Canterbury Tales*, written some 200 years later. A few of them can be seen on the sign of an inn and hotel, The Canterbury Tales, in a street called The Friars, and the city also has a visitor centre of the same name commemorating Chaucer's famous works.

More then 350 years after the Archbishop's death, Becket's shrine was smashed into pieces on the orders of another King, Henry of England, Henry VIII, in defiance of the papal authorities from whom the Archbishop had drawn his support. Now a single candle burns in its place.

The Bishop's Finger, *Canterbury*

The Canterbury Tales, *Canterbury*

Defender of the Faith

The Old King's Head, *Southwark, London SE1*

In his youth Henry VIII was said by his courtiers to have been a handsome man, accomplished in music and sports as well as in the kingly arts of weaponry and warfare; possibly flattery, but probably true. The ancient Greeks used to say, "Those whom the gods love die young", meaning that such men die before their reputation can be tarnished. Certainly Henry would have been a prime example, best remembered now for his obesity, his propensity to behead his wives and statesmen, and his quarrels with Rome.

Born six years after the end of the Wars of the Roses, in which his father won the throne of England for the Tudor dynasty, Henry knew only too well how the consequences of a disputed monarchy could lead to the deaths and suffering of many innocent Englishmen and the ravaging of his country. He was desperate to produce a male heir.

Henry became heir to the throne in 1502, on his brother Arthur's death at the age of fifteen, and on becoming King he married his brother's widow, Catherine of Aragon. Catherine's failure to produce a male heir resulted in their divorce some thirty-one years later. In 1521 Henry VIII had been given the title "Defender of the Faith" by Pope Leo X, a Florentine De Medici who had been made a cardinal at the age of fourteen. Now, some twelve years on, Henry called upon Pope Clement VII to annul his marriage to Catherine. Unfortunately for the King, Clement was at that time under the political influence of Charles V, Catherine's nephew.

Henry failed to secure the Pope's agreement and after almost a thousand years England broke with the Church of Rome. Four months after Henry had secretly married Anne Boleyn, Catherine was sent away from the royal court to be divorced in May 1533. Queen Catherine went into exile. Her daughter, the Lady Mary, remained in England, being declared illegitimate. On 7 September of the same year, at Greenwich Palace, Anne gave birth to a healthy girl, named Elizabeth after her grandmother.

Henry had eight thousand copies of his version of the Bible printed in English, one for every parish church in England. In the churches, statues and pictures of the saints and symbols of God were destroyed, replaced by symbols of the King. The interior walls, made bare, were whitewashed, just as the exterior church walls had been during medieval times. G. K. Chesterton wrote in his poem *The Secret People*:

They burnt the homes of the shaven men, that had been quaint and kind,
Till there was no bed in a monk's house, nor food that man could find.
The inns of God where no man paid, that were the wall of the weak
The King's Servants ate them all. And still we did not speak.

It might be said that the King's destruction of England's heritage of beautiful medieval monastic architecture and its tradition of ecclesiastical hospitality created a void for travellers and merchants and opened the way for a new part of English culture – its magnificent secular inns.

Much of the country, particularly in the North, still held Catherine in esteem and found it hard to come to terms with the imposition of a new religious regime. In the North Yorkshire village of Osmotherley stands an old inn, the Queen Catherine, bearing her sign.

The village, close to Mount Grace Priory, is said to have been named after a grave containing the remains of a boy, Oswald, and his mother. The inn is reputed to be haunted.

The Queen Catherine, *Osmotherley*

The Old Queen's Head, *Chester*

The Three Bulls' Heads, *Newcastle*

Anne Boleyn, portrayed on the sign of the Old Queen's Head in Chester, was crowned Queen on 1 June 1533 and three months later gave birth to Elizabeth, a daughter who would one day rule a powerful England as its last Tudor monarch. But Ann also could not produce a male heir. The disaffected Henry ordered her execution on charges of adultery. On the morning of 19 May 1536 she was beheaded by a single stroke from a swordsman brought over from France.

Her coat of arms, of three bulls' heads, is displayed on the sign of a public house in Percy Street near the Haymarket in Newcastle.

Within a fortnight Henry married one of her ladies-in-waiting, the blonde Jane Seymour. The following year she died after giving birth to Edward, the King's only male heir. When Henry eventually died his body would be buried next to hers.

Court painter Hans Holbein was then sent to Cleves, in the north of modern-day Germany close to the Dutch border, to paint a portrait of the Duke's daughter Anne. Accustomed to pleasing his royal patrons, he no doubt overplayed her looks, and the King was horrified when he saw "The Flanders Mare" in the flesh. The marriage lasted only six months and the fortunate Anne was sent home to live for another seventeen years. But someone had to be blamed. It was Henry's secretary, Thomas Cromwell, who had arranged the marriage, who was beheaded.

The Queens Head, *Stratford-upon-Avon*

Wife number five, Catherine Howard, met the same end as her cousin Anne Boleyn but at the hands of an axe-man.

A black–and–white pub adorned with hanging flower baskets, in Ely Street, bears a sign, "The Queen's Head in Stratford-upon-Avon". It displays the unusual sign of Her Majesty having lost hers.

Having suffered from smallpox as a young man, and later from malaria which affected him for the rest of his life, Henry's personality was changed by two jousting accidents. After the first, at the age of thirty-five, he developed chronic migraines and painful leg ulcers. The second took place on 24 January 1536 at Greenwich Palace, where the forty-four-year-old king was showing off to the ladies. Henry was in full armour when his horse, also in armour, fell on him. He was unconscious for two hours, close to death it was feared, and perhaps suffered a brain injury. In a period of four years his waist increased by seventeen inches. He died on 28 January 1547 at the age of fifty-five amid the stench of his ulcerating leg wounds. His body, resting overnight on the way to Windsor, burst its coffin and sentries found dogs licking his remains.

Henry was survived by two daughters and a son: thirty-year-old Mary, Elizabeth, aged thirteen, and Edward. All three were to rule England, but being male, the nine-year-old Edward became King Edward

VI on his father's death. For three years England was virtually ruled by Edward's maternal uncle, who had been made Duke of Somerset. When he fell out of favour John Dudley emerged as leader. His portrait hangs outside a pub in Newcastle's Clayton Street.

The Duke of Northumberland, *Newcastle*

Dudley was created Duke of Northumberland and managed to stay in control for the rest of the young King's life. Somerset was executed, accused of an attempted coup. When young Edward died at the age of fifteen, Dudley attempted to install his daughter-in-law Lady Jane Grey, the same age as Edward, as his successor. She became the "Nine Day Queen" before she and Dudley met the same fate as Somerset.

During Henry VIII's reign John Dudley had served as a general and an admiral. It was on Dudley's flagship the *Great Harry* that the King dined on the eve of the battle of the Solent in 1545, between Hampshire and the Isle of Wight. The French invading force had been driven off the Isle of Wight and the day before the main battle the navies had exchanged fire at long range. The battle was indecisive and is remembered for the sinking of the *Mary Rose* with the loss of 400 lives. The English version was that incompetent sailors had allowed the ship to list, taking in water. The French claimed to have sunk her with guns from heavily-armed, oar-driven galleys. In 1982 the *Mary Rose* was salvaged and laid to rest in her museum in Portsmouth, where studies have supported the French version of events.

The Gun, Keyhaven

A seventeenth-century inn, the Gun, stands in Keyhaven, amidst the Hampshire salt marshes and overlooking the Solent and the Isle of Wight. In the late nineteenth century it was frequented by soldiers from nearby Hurst Castle, built as part of Henry VIII's coastal defences. Once an important port for the salt trade, Keyhaven is now a quiet village attracting walkers, bird-watchers and yachtsmen, a far cry from the ancient roar of cannons.

Good Queen Bess

The King & Queen, *Highworth*

Elizabeth Tudor lived through the reigns of her half-brother Edward and half-sister Mary, and in Mary's reign had been arrested as an accomplice to treason. Sent to the Tower of London, she had been in serious danger of execution. On 17 November 1668, at the age of twenty-five, the five feet four inches-tall, curly-haired redhead became Queen of England.

The young Queen was an accomplished musician on the lute and keyboards and loved dancing and masques. A skilled horse rider, her favourite outdoor occupations were hawking and stag-hunting armed with a crossbow, and watching the "sports" of dog-fighting, cockfighting and bear-baiting.

King Henry VIII's grave concerns over producing a male heir had been unfounded. Unlike her father, who ruled by fear and brute force, Elizabeth ruled by powers of persuasion. The reign of the Virgin Queen, who gave her name to Virginia, saw England grow as a world power. She spoke of herself and her father: "I may not be a lion, but I am a lion's cub and I have a lion's heart." Father and daughter appear on the sign of the King and Queen in the High Street in Highworth. The coaching inn, said by some to date back 800 years, is the oldest in this Wiltshire town.

Tunnels are said to lead from the inn to the site of a former monastery. The tale is told of a monk who stood trial here in the thirteenth century for breaking his vows and was hanged outside the inn. Stories are also told of the ghostly appearance of a disfigured and hunchbacked monkish figure, no more than four feet six inches tall, gliding across the cobbled yard where the stables used to be.

The sign of the Queen's Head hangs outside an inn in Stow on the Wold, Gloucestershire. It is based on the life-sized portrait of about 1588, attributed to John Gower. Elizabeth used symbolism to promote her virtues; the pearls on the portrait were a sign of her virginity and her favourite black and white symbolised constancy and purity. The oil painting became known as the Armada Portrait, named after Sir Francis Drake's famous victory.

The Queen's Head, *Stow on the Wold*

On 13 December 1577 Francis Drake left Plymouth in his flagship the *Pelican*, ostensibly on a trading mission to the Nile. Queen Elizabeth's secret orders would send him on his greatest adventure. With instructions to raid Spanish colonies on the Pacific coast he set out with four other ships, the *Swan*, the *Christopher*, the *Marigold* and the *Elizabeth*, and a combined crew of 164 sailors, archers, musicians and adventurers. Before rounding the treacherous Cape Horn, Drake ordered the small *Christopher* and the *Swan* to be broken up and the crew and stores to be transferred to his other ships. In the stormy seas the *Marigold* was lost and the *Elizabeth* became separated, finding her own way home back across the Atlantic.

The Globe, *Ludlow*

The *Pelican*, now renamed the *Golden Hind* after the emblem of Drake's sponsor Sir Christopher Hatton, reached the Pacific in September 1578. Drake and his crew returned home via California, the Philippines, Dutch East Indies and Sierra Leone, after a voyage of 1017 days, their ship laden with spices and its ballast replaced by treasure captured from Spanish galleons. Drake had become the first sea captain and first Englishman to circumnavigate the globe. Legend has it that five months after his return he was knighted by the Queen on board his ship at Deptford.

The sign of the Globe in Ludlow celebrates his achievement. It is another ancient inn reputed to be haunted. Jack Hallam's *The Haunted Inns of England*, published in 1972, tells of the ghost of a bewigged and cloaked soldier, Edward Dobson, murdered here while garrisoned at the castle in 1553. Its sighting has been reported on the second floor landing.

While Sir Francis celebrated his fame, the old song *The Jovial Broom Man* celebrated his crew's safe return, and no doubt was sung by many other seamen who falsely claimed to have sailed in the *Golden Hind* in order to impress their drinking companions:

"But here I've now compassed the globe,
Hey jolly broom man,
And I'm returned as poor as Job,
So therefore make me room man.
And now I'm safe returned here,
Hey jolly broom man,
Here's to you with a cup of English beer,
And therefore make me room man."

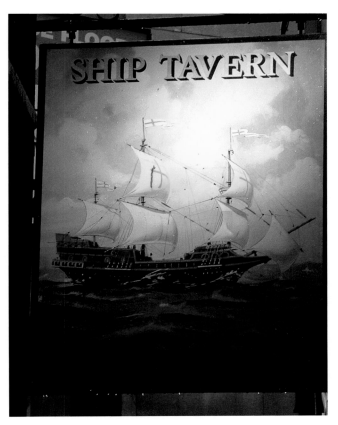

The Ship, *London WC2*

After Drake was knighted, his ship was taken to Deptford and displayed in dry dock for almost a hundred years before it rotted away and was broken up.

The *Golden Hind* is shown on the sign of the Ship Tavern alehouse in Gate Street, off London's Holborn. An inn has been established here since 1549, almost thirty years before the *Golden Hind* began its epic voyage, although the present building dates from 1923. During its early days, in the reign of Henry VIII, it was used for clandestine church services; Catholic priests celebrated the outlawed mass from behind the bar with lookouts posted to warn them and their congregations of the approach of the king's men. The new building still contains some of their hiding holes, but it is said that some of their number were caught and executed in the cellars. Some say their screams can still be heard.

Another sign of the *Golden Hind* hangs outside the Old Thameside Inn in Clink Street, close to where the prison stood, which gave its name, the Clink, to the eternal dictionary of slang. In front of the inn, in St Mary Overie dock, stands a full-size replica of the *Golden Hind*, launched on 5 April 1973. It too sailed round the world, travelling some one-hundred and forty thousand miles before being moored here. It is now used for children's education and as a venue for private and corporate functions.

The Old Thameside Inn, London SE1

The White Bear, Epworth

A white-painted corner pub, the White Bear, stands at the north end of Epworth, the North Lincolnshire village where John Wesley and his brother Charles, founders of the Methodist movement, were born in the first decade of the eighteenth century.

The sign of the White Bear usually represents the arms of the Earls of Kent, but this shows a ship of the Elizabethan Navy, launched in 1563. A financial account records that "painting and colouring red the great new ship called the White Bear" cost the Navy £20, and the carving of "three great personages in wood for the garnishing of the same vessel" cost £1

and 15 shillings. One of the carvings was described as "an image of Jupiter sitting upon an eagle with the clouds, before the head of the ship", and another as "the great piece of Neptune and the nymphs about him for the uprights of the stern".

Weighing 750 tons, she was one of the largest of Drake's squadron of twenty-seven warships and armed merchant ships when he sailed into the port of Cadiz on the afternoon of 29 April 1587 and famously "singed the King of Spain's beard", destroying somewhere between twenty-four and thirty-seven enemy ships. He sailed away with booty of three thousand butts of sherry.

In 1599 the *White Bear* was rebuilt as a fifty-one gunner. She was sold off by the Royal Navy thirty years later.

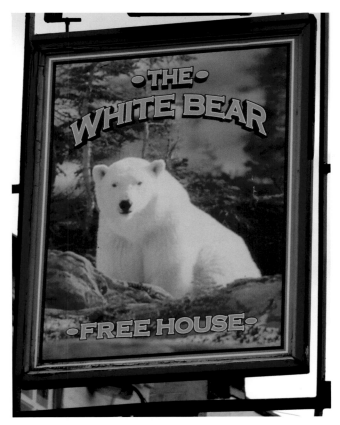

Another take on the White Bear. The sign outside the village pub at Stillington in North Yorkshire shows a polar bear.

The year after Cadiz saw the defeat of the Spanish Armada, at which Drake served as vice-admiral under the command of Lord Howard of Effingham. Drake is credited in popular history as taking the principal role, partly because of the story of his refusal to cut short his game of bowls before boarding ship, and perhaps because during the battle he captured the galleon carrying the pay for the army in the Spanish Netherlands.

Twenty-seven thousand Spanish soldiers were waiting on the Dutch shore ready to cross to England once the crescent-shaped Armada had swept the English ships from the seas. Another nineteen thousand troops sailed on board the 130 Spanish vessels.

With the invaders under orders to land in Kent, and the English defenders gathered at Tilbury in Essex, the consequences of the Armada's victory would have been dire. The English could put out only thirty-six fighting vessels, accompanied by six messenger ships and 143 armed merchant vessels, their confident captains hoping to profit from booty. But the English had some advantages. Unlike the Spanish crews, their seamen were well-trained and their ships, although smaller, were newly constructed, faster and more manoeuvrable, able to evade the Spanish grappling and boarding tactics while firing from a distance at the Armada's huge targets. Only six Spanish galleons were lost in battle but, like the divine kamikaze wind, the typical English summer weather did the rest. Thirty more galleons were too badly damaged to withstand the storms and their wreckage littered the English, Scottish and Irish coasts.

The Spanish Galleon Tavern, in Church Street, Greenwich celebrates the Armada's defeat. Its name was taken from the paintings of the defeat of the Spanish Armada, which were displayed in Greenwich Hospital. In 1873 the hospital became the Royal Naval College.

Sir Francis died of dysentery on 28 January 1596 and was buried at sea off the coast of Puerto Rico. Sir Henry Newbolt's poem *Drake's Drum* tells that in England's greatest time of need the great sea captain will return to the beat of his snare drum, now kept at Buckland Abbey, his Devon home.

"Drake he's in his hammock an' a thousand miles away,
(Capten, art tha sleepin' there below?)
Slung atween the round shot in Nombre Dios Bay,
An' dreamin' arl the time o' Plymouth Hoe!"

The Spanish Galleon Tavern, *Greenwich*

The Lion and the Unicorn

*The **Unicorn** in Lower Corve Street in Ludlow, a seventeenth-century part-timbered coaching inn on the banks of the Wye*

*"The lion and the unicorn were fighting for the crown.
The lion beat the unicorn all around the town.
Some gave them white bread and some gave them brown.
Some gave them plum cake and drummed them out of town."*

This intriguing nursery rhyme is said to date from 1603 when James VI of Scotland succeeded Queen Elizabeth. She left him the debt-ridden kingdom of England and three thousand dresses. The lion was the symbol of England, and as we know, the red lion was Scotland's symbol too. The unicorn was also a symbol of Scotland and the two became united in the royal coat of arms, although the Act of Union did not take place until 1707.

While the red lion was the symbol of the house of Stuart's kingship, the unicorn represented purity and Christ. The Stuarts believed in the Divine Right of Kings, the premise that the monarch was answerable to God alone for his actions, not to his subjects. It led to James's break with the Presbyterian Scottish lowlanders and ultimately to civil war and his son's execution. His portrait is shown on the sign of The Old King's Head, an old inn in Lower Bridge Street, Chester. The building is mainly later seventeenth century, but some parts would have been here when James became King.

The Unicorn, *Canterbury, dating from 1604*

Born in Edinburgh Castle on 19 June 1566, James Charles Stuart became King James VI of Scotland at the tender age of thirteen months. His mother Mary, Queen of Scots had been deposed, suspected of involvement in the murder of his father Henry, Lord Darnley. Suffering from a speech defect and weak limbs, James was in later life crippled by arthritis and gout. However, he had an agile mind and in 1603 was described by Sir Roger Wilbraham as "of the deepest wit and invention". In that year he became King James I of England, having ruled Scotland for thirty-six years. His Danish queen, Anne, gave birth to nine children, although only three survived infancy.

He was the author of many religious works and authorised the King James Version of the Bible in 1604. In the same year James also found time to write his *Counterblaste to Tobacco*, condemning the use of what he called "this filthy novelty".

The Old King's Head, Chester

Hanged, Drawn and Quartered

Remember, remember the fifth of November,
Gunpowder, treason and plot.

On 5 November each year, children and many adults in England celebrate the discovery of the Gunpowder Plot in 1605, an attempt by a small group of disaffected young men to blow up the King and his politicians at the state opening of Parliament.

James VI of Scotland had become James I of England some two years before. On Elizabeth I's death, Protestant England had run out of direct heirs of Henry VIII. Many English Catholics had supported the claim to the English throne by James's mother, Mary, Queen of Scots, and had hoped that the new King would prove more tolerant to their beliefs and allegiances. They were quickly disillusioned.

Robert Catesby was the leading conspirator, but his associate Guy Fawkes, an explosives expert with a military background, has become known as the principal villain. He was the one discovered in Parliament's cellars preparing to ignite the gunpowder barrels that would send the country's government to oblivion and place James's nine-year-old daughter Elizabeth on the throne.

Only a generation ago, children would make straw effigies of Fawkes, dressing him in their fathers' old clothes and wheeling him around the streets asking "Penny for the Guy". They would spend their earnings on fireworks for their celebrations and burn their hapless guys on top of bonfires. These days, in the interests of safety, many public firework displays are held instead.

The Guy Fawkes, York

Fawkes had been born opposite York Minster in 1570 and baptised in the church of St Michael Le Belfry, dwarfed by its neighbour, the largest Gothic church in Northern Europe. On the site of the medieval cottages where he was born is now a pub and hotel bearing his name and image on its sign.

The Hung, Drawn & Quartered, London EC3

The fate of Fawkes and his companions was execution by the barbaric ritual of hanging, drawing and quartering, commemorated by the Hung, Drawn & Quartered (or more correctly hanged, drawn and quartered) pub in Great Tower Street, London, close to where many of these executions took place.

The walls inside display portraits of kings and queens, reminding us that this was the punishment for high treason, and behind the bar hangs a noose.

A sign there displays an abbreviated quotation from Samuel Pepys, who had witnessed the execution of Charles I in 1649 outside London's Banqueting Hall. Perversely, while the attempt by Catholic rebels to kill the king in 1605 had been a heinous act, the execution of his son by the Puritans was celebrated as a glorious victory.

In 1660, on the restoration of the monarchy, all of the rebels except for the regicides, those who signed the King's death warrant, were pardoned. A regicide named Harrison was executed in Pepys' presence on 13 October of that year. The diarist wrote:

To my Lord's in the morning, where I met with Captain Cuttance, but my Lord not being up I went out to Charing Cross, to see Major-general Harrison hanged, drawn, and quartered; which was done there, he looking as cheerful as any man could do in that condition. He was presently cut down, and his head and heart shown to the people, at which there was great shouts of joy. It is said, that he said that he was sure to come shortly at the right hand of Christ to judge them that now had judged him; and that his wife do expect his coming again. Thus it was my chance to see the King beheaded at White Hall, and to see the first blood shed in revenge for the blood of the King at Charing Cross. From thence to my Lord's, and took Captain Cuttance and Mr. Sheply to the Sun Tavern, and did give them some oysters. After that I went by water home, where I was angry with my wife for her things lying about, and in my passion kicked the little fine basket, which I bought her in Holland, and broke it, which troubled me after I had done it. Within all the afternoon setting up shelves in my study. At night to bed.

A small pub stands on a corner of High Street in Huntingdon, native town of Oliver Cromwell, Lord Protector and regicide. This town was also where Samuel Pepys attended the Grammar School in the 1640s, and it is his sign, not Cromwell's, which hangs from the pub.

Son of a London tailor, Pepys attained a BA at Magdalene College, Cambridge, eventually becoming Secretary to the Admiralty and a Fellow of the Royal Society. He is famed for his diary written between 1660 and 1669, containing accounts of the Great Plague and Great Fire of London.

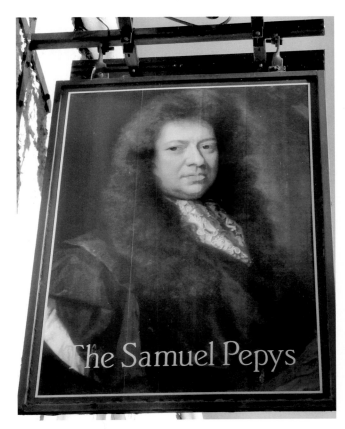

The Samuel Pepys, *Huntingdon*

If I have seen further than others, it is by standing upon the shoulders of giants.

The words "Standing on the shoulders of giants", spoken by Sir Isaac Newton, have been carried around in every Englishman's pockets, appearing on the rim of £2 coins.

Hanged, Drawn and Quartered

England was celebrating Christmas Day 1642 when Newton was born in the village of Woolsthorpe Manor in Lincolnshire. A farmer's son, he attended Trinity College, Cambridge, but his studies were interrupted when the Great Plague caused the college to close for two years. He spent these years back in his native village developing his theories on gravity: every schoolboy knows the story, popularised by Voltaire, of an apple falling on his head.

He returned to Cambridge where he became a professor of mathematics at the age of twenty-six. Among his scientific achievements was the discovery that white light was made up of all the colours of the rainbow, but it was his invention of the reflecting telescope that gained him fellowship of the Royal Society of which he eventually became president. His positions also included Master of the Royal Mint and Whig Member of Parliament for Cambridge University. He died at the age of eighty-four and is buried in Westminster Abbey.

The ancient tree from which the famous apple reputedly fell still stands in the garden of Newton's country home. A cutting taken from it now grows in Cambridge, in front of King's College. Across Magdalene Bridge is the Sir Isaac Newton, its sign inspired by a picture in the National Portrait Gallery painted by court artist Sir Godfrey Kneller in 1702, three years before Newton was knighted by Queen Anne.

The Sir Isaac Newton, *Cambridge*

Roundheads and Cavaliers

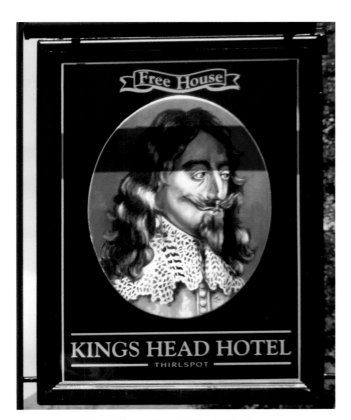

The King's Head Hotel, Thirlspot

Born in Fife on 19 November 1600, Charles Stuart suffered from rickets as an infant and was considered too weak to make the journey to London to attend his father's coronation in 1603. Sensible money was on his popular older brother Prince Henry to inherit his father's throne, but there was to be no King Henry IX. The Prince died of typhoid on 6 November 1612, aged only eighteen, leaving his sickly brother as heir to what his father was first to call Great Britain. Charles became King in 1625.

Three months later he married Henrietta Maria of France, placing a Catholic queen on the throne. Charles himself, influenced by his wife, followed and promoted a "high church" version of Anglicanism, closer to the Church of Rome than many of his subjects would have wished. His religious and political persuasions won him few friends in government and by 1629 he had dissolved Parliament four times, ruling the country virtually alone for the next eleven years.

Having imposed the Anglican liturgy and prayer book on his Scottish subjects, Charles was forced to recall Parliament in 1640 to raise funds to fight the so-called Bishops' Wars north of the border. The following year the news arrived that he also had an Irish rebellion on his hands. By January 1642 civil unrest and rioting in London had forced Charles and his family to leave the capital.

The King's Head in Thirlspot displays his portrait. This Lake District inn claims to have been a coaching inn dating back to the seventeenth century, with a beamed interior and open fires. On the eastern shore of Thirlmere, it is a convenient starting point for climbing Helvellyn and crossing the famous Striding Edge. In the nineteenth century it was simply known as the Thirlspot Inn.

A Saracen's Head, another famous old coaching inn, stands in the centre of the cathedral town of Southwell in Nottinghamshire. Although part of the building dates back to crusading days, the inn was known as the King's Arms until the mid-seventeenth century. Bearing its royal sign, it was visited by Richard I and II, King John, Henry II, the first four King Edwards and James IV of Scotland.

The Saracen's Head, *Southwell*

When Charles I raised the Royal Standard at Nottingham Castle in 1642 to signal the start of the Civil War, he stayed here to avoid the city mobs. After the defeat at Naseby four years later he returned, perhaps sealing the fate of the inn's old name. History tells that in the King's execution an old Saracen sword was used, dating back to the Crusades. The King's Arms was aptly renamed the Saracen's Head.

Today the inn has lost none of its old world charm, its seventeenth-century frontage bedecked with hanging flower baskets. The reception area and restaurant date from 1818 and restoration work in the 1980s uncovered some Elizabethan wall paintings now on display, unlike the inn's ghosts, which remain less conspicuous.

The turning point of the English Civil War was in the north of the country. Here, in the city of York, in Stonegate, the ancient street along which stone was transported from the river to build York Minster, a 'gallows' sign hangs across the narrow street proclaiming the presence of the Old Starre Inn. The inn was set back from the street and in 1733 a house was built in front, hiding it from view. Landlord Thomas Bulman paid rent to the householder opposite to erect his sign, the agreement stating that all of the rent paid had to be spent at the Starre.

Inn signs were growing larger and in the early eighteenth century two people were killed when one fell down into a London street. In 1797 an act of parliament ordered the dismantling of dangerous inn signs, but the Starre's sign survived. The inn might have been named after the Old Star himself, King Charles I. Certainly it was Royalist in its sympathies.

The battle of Marston Moor, the biggest ever fought on English soil, took place on 2 July 1644, near the villages of Long Marston and Tockwith.

In an heroic stand, on that warm summer's evening shrouded in the smoke of twenty thousand muskets, the Royalist Duke of Newcastle's Whitecoat infantry are reputed to have died to a man. Of the heavily outnumbered 17,500 Royalists, about 3,500 were killed, but many tired and wounded survivors somehow managed the seven mile walk to the comparative safety of the city of York. The Starre's cellar was said to have been turned into an operating room and hospital for the wounded by landlord William Foster. Two weeks later York surrendered with honours of war and the Parliamentarian soldiers under the Earls of Leven and Manchester finally gained entrance to the city and to the inn. An old poem makes clear where the landlord's loyalties lay.

A band of soldiers with boisterous din
Filled up the large kitchen of the old Star inn.
Some round the spacious chimney smoking sat
And whiled the time in battle talk and chat.
Some at the brown cake table gamed and swore
While pike and matchlock strewed the sanded floor.
Will Foster, the host, 'mid the group was seen,
With full red face bright eye and honest mean
He smoked in silence in his old inn chair;
No jokes nor jests disturbed his saddened air

Ye Olde Starre Inn, York

To this day, many stories are told of hauntings in the Old Starre Inn, among them the screams of wounded soldiers rising from the cellar from almost four hundred years ago.

Within two years of Marston Moor, the Royalist cause had become hopeless. After a five-month siege Pendennis Castle in Cornwall surrendered on 17 August 1646, the last Royalist stronghold to fall to Cromwell. Near to the castle is the stone-built village of Tregony, home to the King's Arms.

The inn dates from 1615 and it is said that King Charles stayed here on a visit to his supporters at the castle. It stands on the old coaching route between Truro and Falmouth, and still has its arched entrance to the coach yard and Jacobean panelling inside.

Two months before the fall of Pendennis, Charles had already surrendered to the Scots. His grandmother Mary Stuart (Queen of Scots), was beheaded by the English but he would hope in vain for some sympathy from his fellow countrymen.

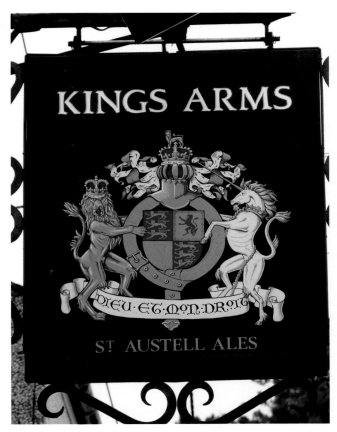

The King's Arms, Tregony

Coffee and Tea

The Old Coffee House, London W1

In London's Beak Street, off Regent Street, stands the Old Coffee House. In spite of its name the house also offers a good range of beers and its friendly interior displays a fascinating collection of old memorabilia. A wealth of brass pots, pans and musical instruments hang from the ceiling; Toby jugs hang from beams, and stuffed animals and birds abound. Upstairs, the dining room is full of Hogarth drawings and old sporting prints, many of horse racing and prizefighting.

In the mid-nineteenth century Thomas Macaulay wrote in his history of England, "The coffee house was the Londoner's home." It was in 1652 that London's first coffee house was opened, by Pasqua Rosee from Turkey. Customers must have been intrigued by the dark new-fangled drink available in the little establishment in St Michael's Alley in Cornhill, and soon the merchant classes adopted such places as their regular meeting houses. Any reasonably dressed man paying the admission charge of a penny could browse the day's newspapers while sipping a dish of coffee, smoking his long clay pipe and seal lucrative business deals with his fellow patrons. Runners would make their rounds of the coffee houses to announce military victories, sales and sailings, and the breaking political scandals of the day.

By 1800 there were 1,400 coffee houses in London, but their days were numbered. An old-established company was to be responsible for the arrival of a new beverage.

The East India Arms, London EC3

For two and a half centuries Britain's trade in the East was dominated by one company, a law unto itself. A plaque outside The East India Arms in London's Fenchurch Street tells its story. Queen Elizabeth I signed a charter on 31 December 1600 creating, "The Company of Merchants of London Travelling to the East Indies". Its first ships arrived in Surat, India, in 1608.

The plaque recounts that more than 200 subscribers invested in what became known as the East India Company, a venture which was granted a monopoly on all English trade to the east of the Cape of Good Hope. At one time a tenth of the British exchequer's revenue came from customs duties on the imports, but Parliament was always wary of the extent of the company's power and influence. Following the Indian Mutiny of 1857 the East India Company was dissolved and the British government took over the administration of India. Lloyds of London took over East India House.

There were vast profits to be made in competing in the tea trade, especially for the owners of the first 'clipper' ships home from the east. Bets were placed on the outcome of the annual tea race, with each ship's progress reported by telegraph and published in the national newspapers.

The famous tea clipper the *Cutty Sark* was built in Dumbarton, Scotland, named and launched on 22 November 1869. With fifteen miles of rigging and a speed of twenty knots, it took twenty-five seamen to sail her with the help of apprentices, some as young as fourteen. Her owner was Jack 'White Hat' Willis, who sported an enormous white top hat and equally impressive long white beard.

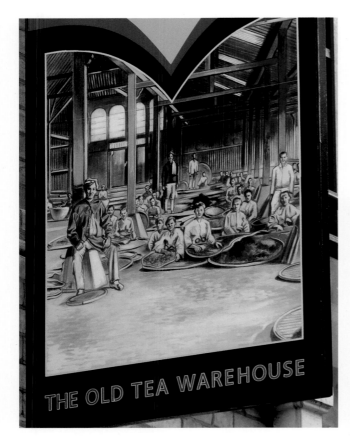

The Old Tea Warehouse *in Creechurch Lane, London EC3, once a warehouse owned by the East India Company.*

Tall enough to 'clip the clouds', clipper ships had been developed in Boston, designed from the fast schooners used to outrun the British blockades in the War of 1812. The first true clipper was launched in the Massachusetts' port in 1833.

The Tea Clipper *in Montpellier Place, London SW7. A plaque outside gives a short account of the tea trade.*

The Cutty Sark, Greenwich

On 16 February 1870 the *Cutty Sark* set sail for Shanghai, the first of her eight voyages to China. It took her 110 days to return with her precious cargo, five days behind the fastest ship. Two years later she competed against the *Thermopylae*, which had set the world record on her maiden voyage. The ships were neck and neck passing Hong Kong, but storm damage put the *Cutty Sark* a week behind. Her crew saw the voyage as a moral victory.

But a week before her launch, the *Cutty Sark's* fate was already sealed; the Suez Canal was opened. The canal allowed only powered shipping to pass through and cut the journey time for steamships by two months.

With the introduction of merino sheep to Australia, the *Cutty Sark* was used for wool transportation and other cargoes. Dogged by bad luck, she suffered a mutiny in 1880 en route to Japan. Her captain walked overboard into the shark-infested Java Sea. In 1916 she was dismasted off the Cape of Good Hope. Her rival the *Thermopylae* was even less fortunate, ending her days in 1907 as target practice for the Portuguese navy.

In 1957 the *Cutty Sark* was opened as a museum ship in Greenwich, the only surviving clipper ship, displaying sixty figureheads, the world's largest collection. Her last piece of ill fortune occurred on 21 May 2007 when a serious fire broke out as she was being restored. Luckily most of her artefacts had been removed.

A few hundred yards downstream on the banks of the Thames stands a Georgian tavern dating from around 1795, now bearing the *Cutty Sark's* sign and name. The busy downstairs bar has wooden and paved floors, bare brick walls partitioned with wooden and glass panels, wooden tables and barrel-styled chairs. A winding wooden staircase leads to more bars upstairs and a dining area with a bay window offering panoramic views across the river.

Now, wha this tale o' truth shall read,
Ilk man and mother's son, take heed:
Whene'er to drink you are inclin'd,
Or cutty-sarks rin in your mind,
Think ye may buy the joys o'er dear;
Remember Tam o' Shanter's mare

So ends the cautionary tale written by the Scottish poet Robbie Burns in 1790 and published the following year. It tells of Tam O'Shanter who, returning home after over-indulging in 'Inspiring bold John Barleycorn', witnesses warlocks and witches performing their rituals. Mesmerised, he watches the young witch Nannie as she begins to remove her clothes down to her 'cutty sark', or short vest, which gave its name to the famous tea clipper. No longer able to contain his enthusiasm he cries out, "Well done Cutty Sark!" He is spotted and flees for home. The inn sign in Lawrence Street in York shows our hero on his grey mare Meg galloping over a stream to escape the clutches of the witches, who could not cross running water. Young Nannie is left holding the horse's tail. She now forms the figurehead of the ship named in her memory.

The inn was originally called the St Nicholas after a nearby church destroyed in the Civil War siege of 1644, but was renamed the Tam O'Shanter in the early 1850s, too early to be connected to the famous racehorse of the same name.

The Tam O'Shanter, York

The Sport of Kings

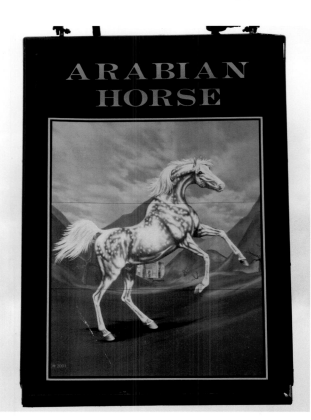

***The Arabian Horse**, Aberford*

Horse racing, the 'sport of kings', dates back in England at least to Roman times. Each year more than five thousand thoroughbreds are born in Britain, all descended from three Arabian horses: The Byerley Turk, foaled in about 1680, The Darley Arabian, foaled in about 1700, and Godolphin, which once belonged to Louis XV of France, foaled in about 1724. Arabian horses were used by Islamic cavalry armies to take North Africa and invade Spain and France. The first to be introduced into England is said to have belonged to James I.

The sign of the Arabian Horse, claimed to be unique, is displayed outside a pub in Aberford. Dating from about 1770, the West Yorkshire pub was originally the Bay Horse. A plaque outside tells us that the name was changed in about 1850 when a string of Arabian horses on their way to Masham were stranded here and people came from miles around to see them.

It also boasts "a lovely restored eighteenth-century fireplace discovered during restoration in 1975, which provides a welcoming huge open fire throughout the winter months".

The picturesque village of Heslington, adorned with daffodils in springtime, is home to the University of York. Its two pubs are well frequented by students. One, the Deramore Arms, is named after the family of Lord and Lady Deramore who for many years lived next door, and was previously the De Yarbrough Arms.

Until 1840, the other went by the name of the Bay Horse. In that year it was renamed the Charles XII after Major Yarburgh's horse had won the St Leger the previous year, walking the thirty miles to Doncaster from its stables which were close to the inn. The first race was a dead heat and the run-off took place later that afternoon. Two days later the horse won the Gold Cup and was sold afterwards for three thousand guineas. It took its name from the Swedish king who defeated the Russians in November 1700 at the battle of Narva, fought in a blinding snowstorm. Russian prisoners outnumbered the whole Swedish army.

While horse racing is called the sport of kings, greyhound coursing is known as the sport of queens. Greyhound track racing, requiring technology, is comparatively modern, introduced in the USA in the 1920s and across the Atlantic a few years later, but for centuries greyhounds have been bred in England as hare coursing dogs.

***The Charles XII**, Heslington*

Greyhounds are believed to have been introduced into Iron Age Britain in the fifth or sixth century BC from the Celtic European mainland. The term grey is probably derived from the Old English word for 'bright', and medieval English nobles had them bred to a vast range of specified colours. They are the fastest dogs, attaining a speed of forty-three miles an hour.

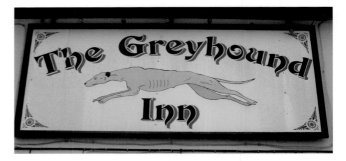

*The **Greyhound** in the market square of Swaffham in Norfolk has been an inn since at least 1830*

*The **Greyhound** in Stockbridge's High Street, a fifteenth-century stone-built inn on the road from London to Salisbury. The Hampshire village claims to be England's fly-fishing capital.*

*The **Greyhound** in Dunnington, an old village inn in the north of Yorkshire. It dates back to the early nineteenth century or earlier.*

Across the Sea to Ireland

On Christmas Eve 1601, outside the medieval wine port of Kinsale in West Cork, a combined Irish, Scots and Spanish force led by Hugh O'Neill was defeated by an English army. With Irish hopes of freedom ended, many emigrated to America and the town is now twinned with Newport, Rhode Island. For the next 300 years Kinsale was a garrison town under English influence, and still contains much Georgian and Victorian architecture.

Its Market Square also contains The Grey Hound pub and bar, which claims to date from 1690, another fateful date in Irish history, when Jacobite forces were defeated on the banks of the Boyne. The English influence is clear. Its ancient-looking inn sign, which seems to depict an Irish wolfhound, is rare in Ireland compared with the more usual ornate Celtic-style frontages of Irish town pubs, and the interior with its wooden partitions, described

The Grey Hound, Kinsale

as 'quaint' by the *Rough Guide to Ireland*, originally came from England.

Within a decade the Irish had repaid the compliment with interest and opened the first Irish pub in England, in London's Fleet Street. It now bears the sign of the Tipperary but had been originally built as the Boar's Head in 1605.

The Tipperary, *London EC4*

A plaque outside tells us that it was built on the site of a beer-brewing monastery dating from 1300, on an island between the River Thames and the River Fleet, which runs under the pub. Built of stone and brick, it survived the Great Fire of London in 1666 while the neighbouring wooden buildings perished in the flames. The plaque goes on to say that the pub was acquired in about 1700 by the Dublin brewery of S. G. Mooney, who furnished it in traditional Irish style. It claims to have been the first pub outside Ireland to sell bottled Guinness.

It took its present name in 1918 from the song *It's a Long Way to Tipperary*, popular during the First World War, but still boasts that it retains its original eighteenth-century character.

A very long way from Tipperary, halfway round the world, Póg Mahone's is a traditional Irish pub in Queenstown on New Zealand's South Island. It boasts a friendly Irish welcome but a less than polite traditional Irish name.

Póg Mahone's, Queenstown, New Zealand

Restoration

The Royal Oak in Evesham, Worcestershire

On 19 October 1781 the British army surrendered with full honours at Yorktown, Virginia, signalling the American colonies' independence. Legend has it that as the seven thousand British soldiers marched away their bandsmen played *The World Turned Upside Down*. The ballad had first appeared in the 1640s as a protest against the Puritan government's banning of Christmas celebrations. A new version of the words appeared in 1660.

> *Cheer up your hearts be not afraid*
> *All you that faithful serve the King,*
> *For though you have long been dismayed*
> *Good News I now intend to bring.*
> *Let sorrows depart and cheer up your heart*
> *And think not on your troubles past.*
> *Let's pray for the King and merrily sing,*
> *Long look't for may now come at last.*

It was on his thirtieth birthday, 29 May 1660, that Charles Stuart arrived in London, welcomed by the joyous multitude, to take his rightful place as Charles II of England.

Some nine years before, following the Royalists' defeat at Worcester, he had hidden in an oak tree while fleeing from his Roundhead pursuers. It was to take him six weeks to reach the Normandy coast.

For some 200 years the anniversary of the return of the King was celebrated as Arbour Day or Oak Apple Day, and since his return many signs of the Royal Oak have graced English inns and taverns.

The King Charles II, an old coaching inn in Broad Street in picturesque Ross-on-Wye, Herefordshire

The Royal Oak *in Tadcaster, North Yorkshire*

Born in 1649 in Rotterdam, James Fitzroy was reputedly the illegitimate son of the exiled Charles II and his mistress Lucy Walters. Lucy had died in 1658, and in 1660 Charles brought his young son across to England, to be created Duke of Monmouth three years later.

With Charles having no legitimate sons, many favoured Monmouth as the King's successor. A plot to kill both Charles and his brother James, placing Monmouth on the throne, failed and the Duke sailed home to his native land. He returned in 1685 on his father's death, when his uncle was proclaimed James II, but the Monmouth rebellion failed with the rebel defeat at Sedgemoor. Monmouth was executed for treason on Tower Hill.

On the old royal mail coach road from Bath to Southampton, about seven miles south of Bath, lies the tiny Somerset village of Norton St Philip. There was once a barn here, owned by the Carthusian monks. It was rebuilt in stone and timber in 1397 as a wool exchange and a guest house for woollen merchants, hosting a weekly market and an annual fair, which must have been a grand event in such a grandiose building.

The original stonework still stands, although the first floor was rebuilt after a fire about five hundred years ago. After Henry VIII's dissolution of the monasteries and his destruction of monastic life, it became one of England's great coaching inns, bearing the sign of St George, patron saint of England and of the crusaders. It was here that the Duke of Monmouth stayed after his defeat at Sedgemoor in 1685. As he stood at an upstairs window, an attempt was made on his life.

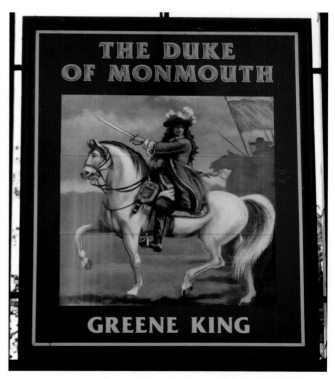

The Duke of Monmouth, *a brick-built early 1930s town pub on Abingdon Road, Oxford*

The George, *Norton St Philip*

Brandy Nan

The Crown & Two Chairmen, London W1

The ceiling in the Upper Hall of the Royal Naval College at Greenwich displays a painting of Victory saluting Queen Anne and her husband George of Denmark. The artist Sir James Thornhill became court painter to George I and was the first English-born artist to be knighted. Father-in-law of William Hogarth, his house and studio were in Dean Street, London.

The Crown and Two Chairmen opposite takes its name from the brave courtiers who carried the Queen's portly frame in her sedan chair, taking their much-needed refreshments here while she attended portrait sittings in Sir James's studio. Nicknamed Brandy Nan, Her Majesty was also partial to the occasional dram.

Today the large bar taking up the frontages in Dean Street and Bateman Street, with its floor of dark wood and large paving slabs, offers the same welcoming atmosphere as it would have done three hundred years ago.

Between 1684 and 1700 the Queen gave birth to thirteen children, none of whom survived into the eighteenth century. She died in 1714, having given her name to Annapolis in Maryland.

A plaque outside the Royal Children in Nottingham tells us that it holds one of the oldest licences in the city. Although the brick and half-timbered corner pub was rebuilt in the 1930s, the licence dates back to the reign of James II when his daughter Anne, then a princess, and her children were in residence in Nottingham Castle. The plaque goes on to tell of the tradition that the royal children were entertained by the innkeeper here and became playmates of his own children.

The Royal Children was one of the first inns to use lamps instead of candles. Inside the pub, at the bar, hangs another sign, now perhaps unique in England. It is a whale's shoulder blade. Shortly after James II's reign, whale oil was introduced as a substitute for candles and this whalebone was displayed outside to advertise that the innkeeper sold oil as well as ale.

The Royal Children, Nottingham

Discovery

The Pier Inn, *Whitby*

And now there came both mist and snow
And it grew wondrous cold
And ice, mast high, came floating by
As green as Emerald.

Written in 1798, Samuel Taylor Coleridge's *Rime of the Ancient Mariner* strikes terror into sailors' hearts.

Outside a stone-built, whitewashed pub in Whitby harbour hangs the sign of the Pier Inn, portraying three famous men of Whitby. Two were father and son, both named William Scoresby. The portrait of the older-looking man is the father, who made his fortune in Arctic whaling. Born in Cropton village on the North York Moors, he came to Whitby in 1779 and sailed as an apprentice on board the *Jane*, some sixty-two years before Herman Melville, author of *Moby Dick*, sailed in a whaler.

The Cod & Lobster, Staithes

The colour portrait on the Pier's sign is of Captain James Cook, born in 1728 in Marton, which was then a small North Yorkshire village. As a teenager he was sent to the fishing village of Staithes to live and work as a grocer's apprentice. Here he would sit at the harbour, outside the Crab & Lobster, listening to the tales of old fisherfolk.

Parts of the inn have been destroyed by storm damage and new defences have had to be built. Inside are old photographs of the town and its fishermen.

With or without his master's permission James left the grocer's shop and walked the thirteen miles to Whitby, where he found work with a Quaker shipowner, John Walker, whose house is now the Captain Cook Museum. Working on the collier fleet, he studied mathematics and astronomy before joining the Royal Navy. Thanks to his navigational and map-making skills he rose quickly through the ranks and was given command of a Royal Society expedition to study the transit of Venus.

His son was born in Whitby in 1789. Young William first sailed with his father at the age of fourteen and his scientific polar explorations gained him a fellowship to the Royal Society of Edinburgh. He went on to write many works, especially on the subject of the earth's magnetism. Named after him are a lunar crater, and possibly Lee Scoresby, the Arctic explorer in Philip Pullman's trilogy *His Dark Materials*.

The ship he chose was the *Endeavour*, a new shallow-draught Whitby collier then sailing under the name of the *Earl of Pembroke*, which was strengthened at Deptford and refitted with an extra exploration deck. Its sign hangs outside a pub in Church Street, Whitby.

The *Endeavour*, with a crew of ninety-four, set sail from Plymouth in 1768 and after rounding Cape Horn stayed in Tahiti for three months to observe the transit. The crew then followed Cook's secret orders to chart the Pacific and sailed to New Zealand, which at first they thought to be the great southern continent. Cook spent the next six months mapping its coastline and naming many landmarks, including Ship's Cove in Resolution Bay, his favourite anchorage and now home to a monument in his honour.

On 19 April 1770 land was sighted on Australia's east coast. Ten days later Cook landed at what he named Stingray Bay. It was later renamed Botanists' or Botany Bay. Four months of charting the Great Barrier Reef ended when the *Endeavour* ran aground in the dangerously shallow waters. The damage and lack of lifeboats forced Cook to return to England, arriving home on 11 July 1771.

Cook's third and last voyage of discovery ended in February 1779 when, at the age of fifty, he was killed by Hawaiian islanders. His remains were buried at sea.

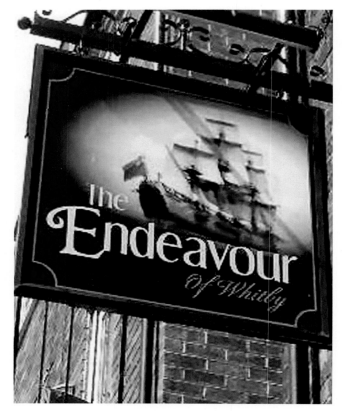

The Endeavour, *Whitby*

Over the Hills and Far Away

The Musketeer, *Boroughbridge*

Over the hills and o'er the Main,
Through Flanders, Portugal and Spain.
Queen Anne commands and we obey
Over the hills and far away

The chorus is from a seventeenth-century song, nowadays known to the tune of *Tom the Piper's Son*, which was adopted and adapted by English soldiers of the Queen. In 1700 Charles II of Spain died, the last of the Habsburg kings. With no heir to the wealthy empire, the French placed their favoured candidate Philip of Anjou on the Spanish throne and the War of the Spanish Succession broke out between the powers of Europe. After thirteen years of fighting it was diplomacy that won the day and Philip V kept his throne, but not before several famous British victories were written into the history books.

The sign of the Musketeer hangs in Horsefair, Boroughbridge, a black-and-white, half-timbered corner pub on the Great North Road. It shows the British uniform as of about 1690: the flat-rimmed felt hat would gradually be replaced over the next few years by the tricorne during Marlborough's so-called 'Lace Wars'.

British possession of Gibraltar prevented French access to the Mediterranean; the necessity of a base enabled a British fleet to winter there. In 1708 the British navy captured the one thousand-strong garrison of Port Mahon in Minorca at a cost of less than fifty casualties. Britain was to keep possession of the island, on and off, for almost a hundred years.

The Port Mahon pub was built in St Clements Street in Oxford two years later, named to celebrate the navy's victory. The present building dates from the 1820s and still retains the original front steps, built to prevent flooding.

At the outbreak of war, John Churchill, Duke of Marlborough, was appointed Commander-in-Chief of the English Forces. He won a string of battles across Europe, his most famous being at Blenheim in 1704 when he marched into Bavaria against the wishes of his Dutch allies and destroyed the French and Bavarian army. Robert Southey's poem *After Blenheim* questions English and French involvement in the Spanish War.

The Port Mahon, *Oxford*

It was the English, Kaspar cried
Who put the French to rout
But what they fought each other for
I could not well make out.
But everybody said, quoth he,
It was a famous victory.

The Bear, Woodstock

Following Marlborough's famous victory the war dragged on for another ten years before being settled, not on the field of battle but in the field of politics. Marlborough had been recalled home in 1711, perhaps too successful for the politicians who sought peace, and his wife Sarah, once Queen Anne's best friend and confidante, having fallen out of favour.

After the War, Blenheim Palace was built as a gift to the Duke. It was to become the birthplace and ancestral home of Sir Winston Churchill. The Palace, now open to the public, is in the village of Woodstock, home to a large and ancient creeper-clad inn known as the Bear. Highly recommended in the *Good Pub Guide*, the inn claims to be 700 years old and to have been host to kings.

Hidden away down Oxford's Blue Boar Street is another Bear, this one claiming to date from 1242. The present building is probably seventeenth century, built next to the original Bear. The *Good Pub Guide* describes it as "Two charming little low-ceilinged and partly panelled sixteenth century rooms" and the Daily Telegraph in its *70 Great British Pubs* as "A quaint relic of a bygone era."

In spite of its age, the Bear's real claim to fame is its collection of ties. Collected from schools, colleges, regiments and clubs since 1954, about five thousand of them hang on every available wall and on the ceiling. Let the visitor beware if he is wearing one not yet in the landlord's collection!

In Colin Dexter's novel *Death is now my Neighbour* his Inspector Morse spent twenty-five minutes here searching in vain for a maroon striped tie to match one worn by a murder victim. He then learnt that he could find a match on the tie rack in the local Marks & Spencer's store.

Dexter wrote thirteen Morse novels but there were thirty-three episodes in the television series starring John Thaw and inspired by Dexter's stories.

The Bear, Oxford

The Long Arms

Eclipsing Morse by some distance is Sir Arthur Conan Doyle's character Sherlock Holmes. The fictional detective was the subject of sixty novels written from 1887 over a period of forty years, beginning with *A Study in Scarlet*. This is complemented by Holmes being the most-played fictional film character (Napoleon is the most played real-life character) with more than seventy actors playing the part in more than 200 films.

Set back from the main road in Northumberland Street, the Sherlock Holmes is a handy watering hole while walking between Trafalgar Square and the London Eye. Originally the Northumberland Arms, the pub stands next door to the Northumberland Hotel used by Sir Arthur Conan Doyle's character Sir Henry Baskerville. The ever-expanding collection of Holmes 'memorabilia' even includes a copy of the detective's will.

The Sherlock Holmes, *London WC2*

On the edge of London's University College, in University Street, Bloomsbury, the Jeremy Bentham Tavern offers a haven for law students and lecturers, local residents and visitors. He was, and still is, the College's spiritual leader. A plaque outside the busy pub tells us that this was once the Lord Wellington, and many customers still refer to it as the "Welly Bar". It was renamed in October 1982 to commemorate the 150th anniversary of Bentham's death.

The plaque continues: "The myth that he was the founder is sustained in a bizarre manner by the college. His 'auto-icon' is in fact his skeleton dressed in his own clothes and topped with a wax model of his head. His real head is mummified and kept in the college vaults. It is brought out during meetings of the college council and he is recorded as being present but not voting. Above the bar can be seen a copy of the wax head made by students at the college. In renaming the pub after him we are reminded of his greatest ideal, 'The greatest happiness of the greatest numbers'. A great man has gone from among us, full of years of good works and of deserved honours in the highest departments in which the human intellect can exert itself. He has not left his equal or his second behind him."

The Jeremy Bentham Tavern, London WC1

A brick-built town pub in Westgate, Lincoln, stands close to the site of the city's gallows before they were moved inside the castle walls. It bears the intriguing name of The Strugglers Inn and the disturbing sign of a victim of the gallows.

Inside is almost a step back into the 1950s with the small Lincoln Snug and a cosy larger bar with a wooden floor and walls covered in prints. Listed in the *Good Pub Guide*, it offers a range of seven good hand-pulled beers.

The Strugglers Inn, *Lincoln*

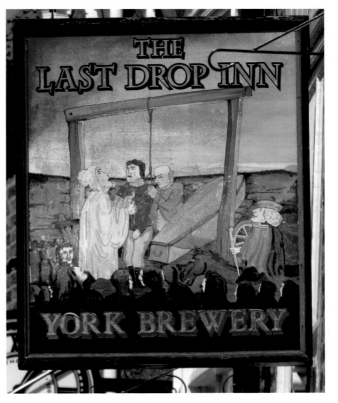

Last Drop Inn, *York*

For many years the bar displayed a stuffed lurcher. It was the pet of one of the pub's regulars, William Clark, and always accompanied him there. While poaching, he inflicted a gunshot knee-wound on a gamekeeper, which proved fatal. In 1877 Clark became the last man to be executed at the castle. After the hanging, the dog remained in the pub pining away for him until it died. Its stuffed carcase was eventually presented to the castle and is now exhibited there.

York Brewery named its first three pubs on the theme of executions. The first, opened in August 2000, is the Last Drop Inn, showing not the last drop of ale but the last drop of life. York was famous for its 'Tyburn', about a mile out on the road from London. Its monument, to those rightly or wrongly executed, stands on the site of the Knavesmire, home to York racecourse. Later executions took place in the castle.

The second opened in 2001 in High Petergate, a stone's throw from York Minster. The sign shows a device cunningly designed to hang three criminals simultaneously. A full-size replica, without the cart, stands in the beer garden at the rear as a warning to unruly customers.

Originally the Wheatsheaf, the brewery's third pub took its name from Peter Rook and Leonard Gaskill, the last two people hanged at nearby Greendykes, executed on 12 May 1676 for stealing thirteen sheep.

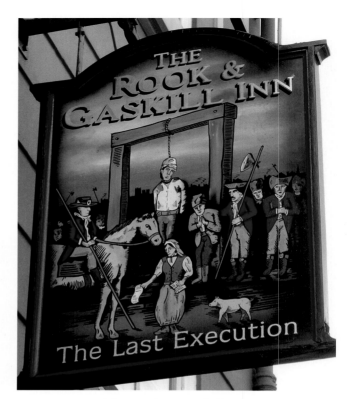

The Rook & Gaskill, York

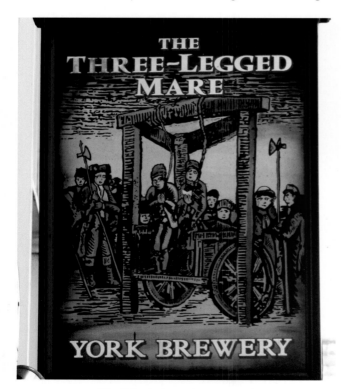

The Three-legged Mare, York

In the Herefordshire town of Leominster, pronounced 'Lemster', an inn displays the sign of the Ducking Stool. Although it shows a town official as the recipient of the ducking, the medieval punishment was normally reserved for women.

The punishment was for witches, prostitutes and scolds, women who gossiped, brawled or were generally a public nuisance. In later witch trials, the stool was dispensed with and the woman was bound thumb to toe and dropped into the water by rope. If she floated she was found guilty and hanged. Unlike in mainland Europe, where it was often the custom to burn witches, burning in England was normally reserved for heretics, preparing them for their fate in Hell's fiery furnace.

Hidden behind London's Strand, in narrow Carey Street, stands a remarkable pub bearing a remarkable date, having somehow survived the Great Fire of London. The sign is an intriguing one. In some cases it is taken as a constellation such as the Plough, and sometimes from the Virgin Mary's celestial crown. Also it can be a Masonic emblem, the meaning of which would be to reveal the sacred arcane. Tradition has it that this one in Carey Street is taken from the seven provinces of the Netherlands because of the Dutch sailors who at one time settled nearby and gave their custom to the inn.

The Ducking Stool, *Leominster*

The Seven Stars, *London WC2*

The Wig & Pen, *Truro*

Best accessed along lanes running behind the Royal Courts of Justice, the entrances to the small front bar are marked Private Counter and General Counter. The private area was perhaps once reserved for members of the legal profession, needing to discuss their work away from the busy court. Indeed, as one of the front window displays reminds us, part of the pub used to be a wig shop supplying these lawyers with their customary headgear.

As a fashion accessory the wig, full of ringlets and curls, came to England from France. In order for it to fit, hair had to be cropped or the head shaved. Samuel Pepys adopted the fashion in 1664, and wearing it in church for the first time noted in his diary that he "Did not prove so strange to the world as I was afeared I would". Nevertheless he complained of catching a cold through having to remove it so often, one caught fire, and he found a new one delivered to him to be full of nits. The next year, sales in London plummeted, customers suspecting that many had been made from the hair of victims of the Great Plague. As the headgear regained popularity, wig-snatching became common and children were warned not to go out alone in case thieves cut off their hair to sell to wig makers.

The Wig & Mitre in Lincoln stands at the top of the aptly-named Steep Street, halfway between the castle's Crown Court and the cathedral, each only a few hundred yards away. It sports two double-faced signs, one side showing a lawyer and the other a bishop. The small frontage belies the size of the pub's interior which goes through into Drury Lane opposite the castle. It also has a bar and large seating areas upstairs. Some of the pub is modern, having been renovated in the 1970s, but parts of the building date back to the fourteenth and sixteenth centuries. It became the Wig & Mitre in 1977.

*The **Tilted Wig** in Warwick, a listed Georgian structure and one of the town's oldest pubs with a licence dating back to an earlier building in 1694. The sign implied that members of the judicial profession could relax here.*

The Wig & Mitre, Lincoln

The Wig & Mitre, Lincoln

The Georgians

The George, *Penrith*

Born in Hanover in 1660, nine days before Charles II was restored to the English throne, Georg Ludwig would not have expected to be one of his successors. But some forty years later the English Parliament passed the Act of Settlement, declaring that his mother Sophia would succeed Queen Anne. In 1714, at the age of eighty-three, Sophia died. Three months later, following Queen Anne's death, Georg Ludwig found himself George I of England, first of the Hanoverian dynasty which would rule the vast British Empire until 1901.

His reign was to last until 11 June 1727, when he died during a visit to Hanover, leaving his son to become George II. Both during and after his life many old English inns were named in his honour.

The George in Penrith, Cumbria, is a large Georgian-fronted coaching inn on the London to Glasgow mail route. It dates from the eighteenth century or earlier, when it would have borne a different name.

Also in Cumbria, in the picturesque Lake District, is the George in Keswick. A black-and-white inn in St John's Street, it is described in the *Good Pub Guide* as a traditional old place with an attractive black-panelled side room, open-plan main bar and Elizabethan beams.

The George, *Keswick*

While the Gentlemen Go By

It seems strange that a German king should find his way onto an English inn sign, but on the quayside at Fowey in Cornwall stands the King of Prussia. This is Frederick II of Prussia, Frederick the Great, grandson of George I of England. He became a popular figure during the Seven Years War of 1756-63 because of his alliance to England against the French.

His palace of Sanssouci, now a world heritage site and almost a rival to Versailles, stands in Potsdam in Brandenburg. As Brandenburg was within the Holy Roman Empire, the Hohenzollern rulers were unable to call themselves kings here, but their eastern possessions in Prussia were outside the Emperor's jurisdiction.

But the sixteenth-century inn visited by Sir Francis Drake, and later by Oliver Cromwell, has another sign. This is of John Carter, an infamous Cornish smuggler, known as Black Jack Carter. Born in 1770, he acquired the nickname King of Prussia as a boy while playing soldiers. Until 1807 he operated near the village of Marazion in a cove called Port Leah, which was renamed Prussia Cove in his memory. The cove was the setting for the film *Ladies in Lavender* starring Dames Judi Dench and Maggie Smith.

If you wake at midnight, and hear a horse's feet,
Don't go drawing back the blind, or looking in the street,
Them that ask no questions isn't told a lie.
Watch the wall my darling while the Gentlemen go by.

Rudyard Kipling's *Smugglers Song* goes on to describe five and twenty ponies trotting through the dark with smuggled goods for eager customers in every walk of life.

The King of Prussia, Fowey

The King of Prussia, Fowey

Perhaps the most famous English establishment known for smuggling, the remote grey-stoned Jamaica Inn stands on stark and windswept Bodmin Moor. It may well have been named after the Jamaica rum which smugglers traded here. There is said to have been a Jamaica Inn built here in 1547, but the present building dates from 1750, built along the old coaching route through West Cornwall to provide a posting house where horses were changed. Shepherds and travellers shared the warmth of the timber fires here, along with highwaymen who would follow the coaches to rob the passengers.

John Burton, a china and glass salesman from Falmouth, had occasion to spend Christmas Eve

The inn's fame arose mainly from Daphne du Maurier's novel, published in 1936 and later made into a film. It has a Mary Yellan's bar named after the heroine and a Joss Marlin's bar named after the villain. The novel is set in the days when most of England's smuggling took place on the coasts of Devon and Cornwall. Only twenty miles by pack horse from Cornwall's north and south coasts, the inn was a smuggler's haven. An 'honest' cartman would take the contraband goods along the track to be sold on further inland.

Locals tell of a ghostly sailor, dressed in a long cloak and tricorne hat, who sits on a low wall outside. Drinking in Mary's Bar, he was called away by a mysterious stranger and found dead on the moor. He is said to return to finish his drink. His murderer was never caught.

The Rum Runner stands on a corner in Wharf Road, Retford. It was known as the Ship until 2001. The weathered sign shows a young man running with a barrel on board ship. It tells us that rum-running was the smuggling of goods over water, the overland equivalent being known as bootlegging.

The Jamaica Inn, Bolventor

here in 1853 and wrote that he found the taproom full of "a lot of old boozers, principally moor men". They included the gypsy fiddler Billy Lee, Boswell the rat catcher, local drunk Billy Peppermint, and a "doggish cove who was wearing a waggoner's braided smock frock" and who sang a song of Brannan the highwayman, the Irish 'Brennan on the Moor' revived by the famed Clancy Brothers in the 1960s.

The Rum Runner, *Retford*

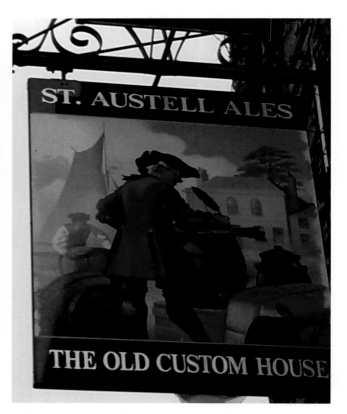

The Old Custom House, *housed in the old Customs and Excise listed building on the South Quay of the Cornish fishing village of Padstow. It is now a hotel boasting luxurious accommodation, Pescadou Restaurant and a fine range of beers.*

By Battle and by Pot

The Ship & Shovell, *London WC2*

The Ship & Shovell stands in Craven Passage, off Craven Street in London. The *Good Pub Guide* tells us that it was formerly a coal-heavers' pub called the Ship and Shovel, but with the changed spelling the sign shows the early eighteenth-century admiral Sir Cloudesley Shovell. He lived close by in May Place, although the pub was not built until some thirty years after his death.

The admiral was born in Norfolk in 1650, and joined the navy at the age of thirteen to rise through the ranks. He was involved in the taking of Gibraltar in 1704 and soon afterwards became Commander of the Fleet. Returning from an unsuccessful attack on Toulon in the late autumn of 1707, he ran part of his squadron aground off the Scilly Isles, losing all 800 crew of his flagship HMS *Association* and 1,400 men in total. The admiral was barely alive when he was swept ashore, and some years later a local woman confessed on her deathbed to having murdered him for his emerald ring.

A maroon and white-painted double-fronted pub in the North Yorkshire fishing village of Staithes bears the sign of the *Royal George*, an eighteenth-century warship. It was the flagship of Admiral Richard Kempenfelt, whose Swedish father had served in the British army. Richard joined the Royal Navy and saw active service in the West and East Indies before being promoted to rear admiral in 1780. Outnumbered by the French, he won the battle of Ushant in 1781. The following year he hoisted his flag on the *Royal George*.

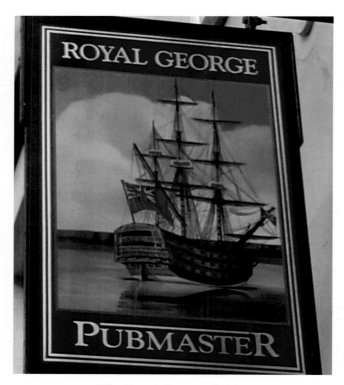

The Royal George, *Staithes*

With orders to sail to the relief of Gibraltar, he called at Portsmouth harbour for a hasty repair to a water pump three feet below sea level. On 29 August the guns were moved across the decks to allow the ship to list, but it was caught by a sudden breeze and keeled over, with many tradesmen, women and children on board as well as the crew. More than 800 people were drowned including Kempenfelt, who was trapped in his cabin. Survivors numbered only about 230. William Cowper commemorated the tragedy in his poem *On the Loss of the Royal George* which ends:

> *But Kempenfelt is gone,*
> *His victories are o'er,*
> *And he and his eight hundred*
> *Shall plough the wave no more.*

The Defeat of the Floating Batteries, subject of an oil painting by the American John Singleton Copley, commissioned by the City of London, depicts an incident at Gibraltar in the same year. The spectacular work measures more than twenty-five feet across and twenty-two feet high, featuring life-size figures of British and Hanoverian officers with horse and cannon, and hangs in the art gallery of London's Guildhall. It shows the French and Spanish forces launching their 200 guns to bombard the British colony, which had been won by the treaty of Paris eighteen years earlier.

The General Eliott, Leeds

The British replied with red-hot cannonballs, setting fire to the batteries, causing them to explode.

Credit for the successful defence went to the Governor of the colony, General George Augustus Eliott, who became first Baron Heathfield. His portrait is the subject of numerous inn signs, this one most likely based on a painting by Sir Joshua Reynolds. Robert Graves' poem *General Eliott* muses that he is better known on inn signs than in history:

> *And paint shall keep his buttons bright*
> *Though all the world's forgot*
> *Whether he died for England's pride*
> *By battle, or by pot.*

A pub in the North Yorkshire town of Boston Spa displays the portrait of Admiral Sir Edward Hawke, based on an oil painting by Francis Cotes. The painting, which hangs in the National Maritime Museum, shows the Admiral in front of the rocky landscape of Quiberon Bay in north-west France. It was here that he won his most famous victory in the evening twilight of 20 November 1759.

Under orders to blockade the French coast, Hawke intercepted the French fleet twenty miles out to sea on its way to join the troop ships. In a howling gale, the French took refuge in the bay, expecting Hawke to call off the chase. Hawke took the risk, entering the dangerous waters, and among the rocks and reefs he had his adversary trapped. The French lost half of their ships and two-and-a-half thousand of their best seamen, and with them was lost the chance to invade England.

> *Ye mariners of England*
> *That guard our native seas*
> *Whose flag has braved a thousand years*
> *The battle and the breeze*

The Admiral Hawke, Boston Spa

The Jolly Sailors, *overlooking Whitby harbour*

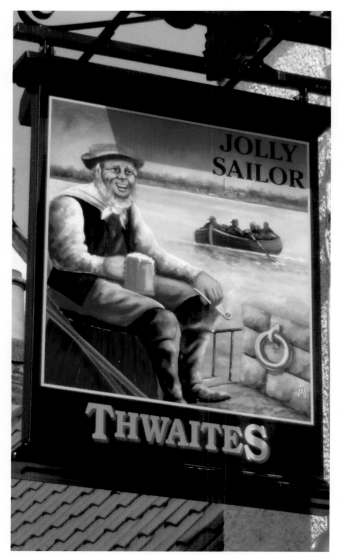

The Jolly Sailor, an inn on the banks of the Ouse in Cawood, North Yorkshire. A lone river sailor enjoying his beer would have presented an easy target for the press gangs.

Thomas Campbell's poem praises the men who crewed the ships of the Royal Navy through the ages. In 1793, on the outbreak of the Napoleonic Wars, the navy numbered some forty-five thousand men. The following year it rose to eighty-five thousand and by 1799 had reached one hundred and twenty thousand. The sailor's life was far from jolly. Some volunteered to take advantage of the navy's protection against creditors and the debtors' prison. The volunteer took the king's shilling and was 'imprest' into the king's service. Sometimes he was tricked, drinking from a tankard into which a shilling had been dropped by a recruiting officer. Only by drinking from a glass-bottomed tankard could he be sure of his freedom.

During wartime it was particularly difficult to recruit. The Impress Service, commonly known as press gangs, were given the task of rounding up sailors aged between eighteen and fifty-five and impressing them. They became feared throughout England, capturing any likely-looking candidate who came within their grasp. His only escape was to call upon his friends to fight them off, or bribery. Once on board ship, on the high seas, he was virtually imprisoned.

The Time of France

The Lord Nelson, *Burnham Thorpe*

Lord Horatio Nelson was born on 29 September 1758 in the rectory of Burnham Thorpe, a tiny village in the north of Norfolk, the sixth of eleven children. His birthplace is long gone but the village inn, known as the Plough until 1807, proudly bears his name and portrait. In its selection of *70 Great British Pubs* the Daily Telegraph reported: "Time seems to have stood still as you enter a bar with flagstone floors and ancient settles."

Nelson was a small and sickly child, but on New Year's Day 1771 he joined the navy at the age of twelve. In spite of his seasickness, from which he suffered for the rest of his life, he was soon appointed midshipman by his maternal uncle, seeing action as a teenager in the West Indies during the American War of Independence. By the age of twenty he had been promoted to the rank of captain. He lost the sight of his right eye in an action on land with the army, and two years later, at Santa Cruz de Tenerife, he lost his right arm. Through his daring and inventiveness he rose rapidly through the ranks and by 1797 he had become a rear admiral and a Knight of the Bath. His ability to inspire his men gave rise to the phrase 'The Nelson touch'.

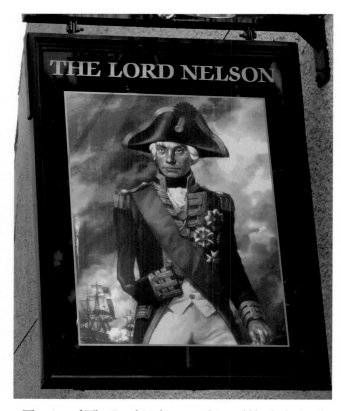

The sign of **The Lord Nelson**, *a white pebble-dashed pub on the edge of the North Yorkshire market town of Thirsk, overlooking St James's Green. It was listed under its present name in 1822.*

He recovered well enough to take part in the Battle of the Nile, commemorated in Felicia Hemans' poem *Capablanca*, which begins:

> *The boy stood on the burning deck*
> *whence all but he had fled.*
> *The flame that lit the battle's wreck*
> *Shone round him o'er the dead.*

The boy Capablanca was the twelve-year-old son of a French naval officer, watched by the spellbound British sailors as he stood alone amidst the flames on board the French flagship *L'Orient*, refusing to leave his post without orders. As the fire spread towards the powder magazines the British drew away. At ten o'clock on the evening of 1 August 1798, in Aboukir Bay, the flagship was ripped apart in an explosion that could be heard twenty miles away. The British picked up some seventy survivors from the crew of five hundred and for twenty minutes the two thousand guns of Nelson's navy fell silent. The victorious Nelson withdrew to Naples and was made Baron Nelson of the Nile.

Sent to fight the Danes, he was victorious at Copenhagen where he famously put a telescope to his blind eye to avoid seeing the French ships he had been ordered to evade. He then sailed to the West Indies, and between 1803 and 1805 he blockaded the French ports. By this time he had become a national hero.

required that the two fleets would engage alongside each other, in line, but Nelson's plan was to approach at right angles and cut his enemy's line in half.

Within two hours Nelson was mortally wounded by a musket ball. It is said that his body was deposited in a captured barrel of French brandy to be preserved for burial in St Paul's Cathedral. The sailors on board the *Victory* climbed down into the hold and used straws to sip from the barrel in what has become known as "tipping the Admiral". They would perhaps have preferred rum.

***The Norfolk Hero**, an inn dating from the mid-nineteenth century in the Norfolk town of Swaffham. The portrait is from a painting by Lemuel Francis Abbott.*

England expects that every man will do his duty

Nelson's message was signalled by flags from HMS *Victory* at 11.45 on the morning of 21 October 1805. His twenty-seven ships of the line faced the French and Spanish fleet of thirty-three. Tactics of the day

***The Lord Collingwood**, Upper Poppleton*

The Admiral's coffin was made from the wood of a French warship. The largest state funeral ever to be held included a four-hour service in St Paul's to which a male-only congregation was invited.

As Nelson lay dying his old comrade and close friend Cuthbert Collingwood took over and brought Nelson's orders to a successful conclusion. He had sailed with Nelson to the West Indies in the two years before Trafalgar and accompanied him in the French blockade. He died at sea near Minorca on board HMS *Ville de Paris* on 7 March 1810, surviving Nelson by five years.

The Lord Collingwood in Upper Poppleton near York displays his portrait. It is taken from an oil painting by Henry Howard which now hangs in Greenwich Hospital.

With such real-life heroes, one wonders why it was necessary to invent more, but invent them they did. C. S. Forester's Horatio Hornblower of the King's Navy was born on the day America won its independence, the son of a Kentish doctor, and given a classical education. By the time we are introduced to Hornblower he is already a captain with the good fortune to share his first name with Lord Nelson. Within eleven novels he has risen in rank, through his daring exploits against the French.

The Admiral Hornblower, Oakham

The sign of the Admiral Hornblower in Oakham High Street, outside a converted seventeenth-century farmhouse in the tiny county of Rutland, hails the sailor's success. Winston Churchill was one of his many admirers.

Nelson's rival to fame in the Napoleonic wars was Arthur Wellesley, who became The Duke of Wellington, Prime Minister, and a favourite subject of inn signs. These two individuals are the only two commoners to feature in the Inn Sign Society's top twelve signs. Nelson was an Englishman but his opposite number was born in Ireland, in County Meath in 1769.

His first military action was against the French in Flanders, and in 1786 he moved to India where, a year later, his brother became Governor General. After a brilliant victory in the Mysore War, at Assaye in 1803, he came back to England where he was knighted and became a Member of Parliament.

*The **Wellington Arms** in Burton on Trent. The sign is based on an 1812 portrait by Francisco da Goya which hangs in the National Gallery.*

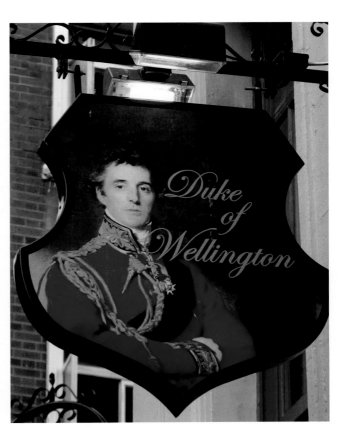

*The **Duke of Wellington** in Winnett Street, London W1. The sign is based on a painting in 1815 by Sir Thomas Lawrence, displayed in the Victoria and Albert Museum.*

The Waterloo Arms, Lyndhurst

For a time Sir Arthur was Chief Secretary for Ireland but he was recalled to active service in the Peninsular War and in 1808 took command of the British, Portuguese and Spanish armies. His string of victories brought him the title of Duke of Wellington in 1814 and, with Napoleon safely exiled on the island of Elba, he was appointed ambassador to France.

By this time it seems that the Duke had become the most popular military man on England's inn signs, although his contemporary Lord Byron warned of transient glory:

> *Vernon, the butcher Cumberland, Wolfe, Hawke,*
> *Prince Ferdinand, Grandby, Burgoyne, Keppel, Howe,*
> *Evil and good have had their tithe of talk*
> *And filled their sign-post then, like Wellesley now.*

Napoleon's escape led to Wellington's greatest battle on 18 June 1815 at Waterloo, not far from Brussels. Marginally outnumbered by the French, his forces held out until the arrival of his Prussian allies, who had been beaten by the French only two days before. He said of the engagement at Waterloo that it was "the nearest-run thing you ever saw in your life."

Casualties, killed and wounded were estimated at forty-seven thousand. At a time when dental care was virtually unknown, the bodies of these young fallen provided military surgeons with many sets of false teeth, known in England for years afterwards as 'Waterloos'.

The Waterloo Arms stands outside Lyndhurst, Hampshire, a thatched seventeenth-century inn on the edge of the New Forest. Its sign is based on Robert Alexander Hillingford's painting *Wellington at Waterloo*, the original landscape format showing the Duke urging one of his infantry squares to stand firm in the face of a French cavalry charge.

The Marquis of Anglesey pub can be found in London's Bow Street. Born Henry William Paget in 1768, the Marquis became Lord Uxbridge in 1812.

He commanded the British cavalry and horse artillery at Waterloo, personally leading the charge of heavy cavalry. He lost a leg in the closing stages of the battle. It was buried in a garden at Waterloo with its own gravestone. The Victorian journalist, reporter and poet Thomas Gaspey wrote of the Marquis:

And now in England, just as gay
As in the battle brave
Goes to the rout, review, or play
With one foot in the grave.

The Marquis of Anglesey, *London WC2*

Perhaps the best-known fictitious account of Wellington's battles is told through the exploits of Bernard Cornwell's Sharpe of the 95th Rifles Regiment. Hornblower and Sharpe both rose through the ranks to become intrepid commanders but had very different backgrounds, Sharpe having risen from the gutters of London. A sign outside the Volunteer in St Catherine's Square, in the Gloucestershire market town of Chipping Campden, shows an English infantryman of the Napoleonic Wars. Listed as the Rifle Volunteer in 1867, the inn was once a recruitment centre.

The term 'volunteer' was often a euphemism as many of Wellington's men had little choice but to serve their king and country on the battlefield. The 'Iron Duke' is said to have called them the 'scum of the earth'. The redcoat was recruited from all walks of life, but usually from the deprived bottom rung of the social ladder, among them the common criminal serving out his sentence in the front line of battle. Rudyard Kipling's barrack room ballad pleads the common soldier's case, despised by civilians but expected to die for his flag.

It's Tommy this, and Tommy that,
And Tommy 'ow's yer soul?
But it's thin red line of heroes
When the drums begin to roll.

The Volunteer, *Chipping Campden*

The Blues

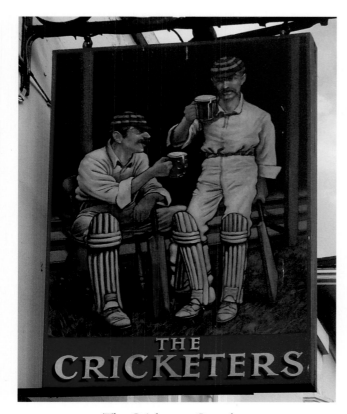

The Cricketers, *Canterbury*

Wellington was reported to have said that, "Waterloo was won on the playing fields of Eton." He probably said no such thing, as the elite Berkshire public school had no proper playing fields when he was a pupil, but it suited the Etonians to be considered the founding fathers of English discipline and the stiff upper lip, the quotation being revealed only after the Duke had died. Some football was played there, with few rules and certainly plenty of fighting, and also the gentlemanly game of cricket.

The sign of the Cricketers in St Peter's Road in the centre of Canterbury shows the game how many believe it should be played, in whites, over three days, perhaps five, constantly interrupted by the English summer's frequent showers of rain. The corner pub also displays a striking, colourful wall sign, 'Shepherd Neame & Co. Brewers since 1698'.

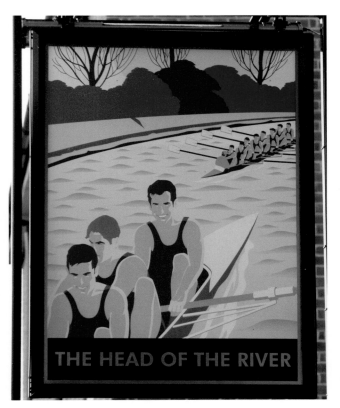

Eton, England's first public grammar school, had been founded in 1440 by Henry VI for twenty-five poor scholars. Four months later he founded King's College, Cambridge, the first of the university's thirty-two colleges. It was England's second university, following Oxford. Oxford had become a seat of learning in 1167 when English students gathered there after Henry II banned them from attending the university in Paris.

The Cricketers Arms, *Oxford*

*Oxford's **The Head of the River** shows the rowing 'eight' in the university's dark blue. Originally a nineteenth-century warehouse, it was a storage house for boats until it was converted into a pub in 1977.*

The first university boat race took place at Henley-on-Thames in Oxfordshire on 10 June 1829, between Oxford and Cambridge universities, the first ever inter-collegiate competition. The Oxford team won, wearing the dark blue colours of Christ College. The

The Cambridge Blue, Cambridge

Cambridge crew wore red sashes, but for the second race in Westminster seven years later their boat carried the light blue ribbons of Eton. Since 1856 the 'Varsity' boat race has become an annual event watched by two hundred and fifty thousand spectators along the 4 miles and 374 yards of the London banks of the Thames between the bridges of Putney and Mortlake.

The King Street Run, *Cambridge*

By the 1860s, 'blues' were also being awarded by both universities for students selected for first-team cricket and athletics. Now they are awarded to men and women for a wide range of sports including rugby union, football and tennis, but the boat race still holds the highest profile.

Another sport, involving a running race and a little more besides, is indulged in by students every two years in Cambridge's King Street, in spite of attempts by the university fathers to have it banned. Known as the King Street Run, it involves a pint of beer taken at every pub en route in a dash to be first to finish. At one time there were at least seven pubs as obstacles; now there are fewer, but one still bears the event's name as its sign. Another of these obstacles, the Champion of the Thames, displays sound advice to participants. Its sign reads, "This house is dedicated to those splendid fellows who make drinking a pleasure, who reach contentment before capacity and who, whatever the drink, can take it, enjoy it, and still remain gentlemen".

Lessons in the art of peaceful drinking might have been learnt from an incident in Oxford in 1355. On St Scholastica's Day, 10 February, two students at the Swindlestock Tavern complained about the quality of ale. One threw a tankard at the landlord, who demanded their arrest, but their colleagues turned out to defend them. Riots over the next two days resulted

Champion of the Thames, *Cambridge. Prior to being a pub, this unusually named Cambridge hostelry was the private residence of a prize-winning rower whose post would come addressed 'Champion of the Thames, King Street, Cambridge'.*

in about a hundred deaths, mostly students. Edward III ordered the townspeople to do penance and to pay an annual fine of sixty-three pence – a penny for every student killed. Fermenting the animosity between 'town and gown', the fine was paid for the next 470 years.

The last of Thomas Hardy's novels, *Jude the Obscure*, tells the story of the working class Jude Fawley who dreams in vain of becoming a splendid fellow at Christminster, a fictional city modelled on Oxford. Hardy tells of Jude's failed marriage and his relationship with his cousin Sue Bridehead. The novel, published in 1895, was condemned as offensive to Victorian morals and was publicly burnt by the Bishop of Exeter in the same year.

A brick-built pub in Oxford's Jericho district and once called the Prince of Wales, it now goes by the novel's name and shows the sign of a young man, perhaps more akin to Dick Whittington, approaching the city of dreaming spires.

Oxford's Tom Tower is home to Great Tom, known locally as Old Tom, the city's loudest bell. Its name commemorates Thomas Wolsey, founder of Christ Church College. Close by, in St Aldates, is a small pub also known as the Old Tom.

Jude the Obscure, Oxford

Bunter's Bar in Truro, Cornwall, named after Frank Richards' creation, the much-loved Billy Bunter of Greyfriars School. The stories were part of the Magnet Library series published from 1908 to 1940. The novels also featured the notorious bully Flashman.

In olden times the bell was rung 101 times at five minutes past nine each evening, the time the gates closed, to announce that each of Oxford's 101 students was safely inside. Oxford now has more than twenty thousand students but fortunately the tradition is preserved each evening by ringing only the original number of times.

The Old Tom, Oxford

When This Old Bowl Was New

The George in Easingwold, North Yorkshire, a coaching inn about halfway along the old London to Edinburgh mail route, with its sign of King George III.

George III is best remembered by many through the 1994 film *The Madness of King George* starring Nigel Hawthorne as the King and Helen Mirren as Queen Charlotte. During the King's illness he stayed in Queen's Square in Bloomsbury, an area famous for its hospitals and named after Queen Anne, who died in 1712 while the square was being built.

During his time here he was treated privately by Dr Willis. Meanwhile, Queen Charlotte rented a small cellar beneath a nearby alehouse in which she stored delicacies for her husband.

Later during the King's reign the alehouse was named the Queen's Larder in honour of Charlotte. In 1930, Thomas Burke in his *English Inns* said that it had the frugal but welcome appearance of a village inn looking out onto the trees in Queen's Square. A plaque outside the building tells of its history.

The Queen's Larder, London WC1

The ancient abbey in Whitby overlooks the grey North Sea. It was on this site, in the year 664, that a synod was called to unite the Northumbrian and Roman churches. 199 steps lead down from the abbey to the Duke of York, a grand old pub overlooking the harbour and adorned with the old photographs by Frank Meadow Sutcliffe amongst its memorabilia. It was the local inn of Bram Stoker, whose Count Dracula was inspired by the old churchyard beside the abbey.

The Duke, whose portrait appears only on one side of the sign, was Frederick, son of George III. He had been born on 16 August 1763 in St James's Palace, the eleventh of fourteen Dukes of York, a title given to the monarch's second eldest son. Six of them later became kings of England. Frederick married Frederica

The Duke of York, *Whitby*

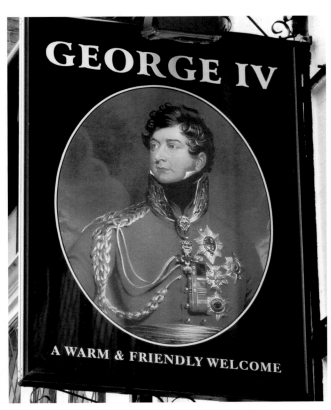

The George IV in Bore Street, Lichfield. The portrait is from an enamel miniature painted by Henry Bone in 1819, while George was Prince Regent.

Charlotte of Prussia but they separated and had no children. He was rumoured to have fathered several illegitimate children, none of whom inherited his title. Prince George became Prince Regent when his father George III was declared insane. In his youth he seems to have gone out of his way to upset his father, secretly marrying a Catholic and supporting the Whig party, while the King favoured the Tories (each party was named after Scottish and Irish bands of brigands).

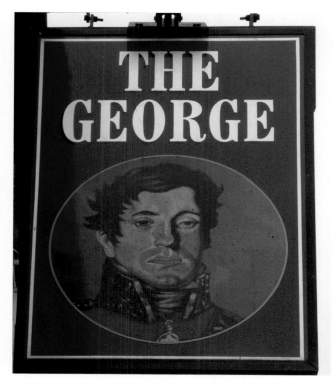

The George, *a mock Tudor-style pub in Market Rasen, a small Lincolnshire town famous for horse racing*

In 1795 George officially married Caroline of Brunswick, persuaded to do so by Parliament in exchange for it relieving him of his debts. His treatment of his new wife made him unpopular. They soon separated, and on becoming King in 1820 he tried unsuccessfully to divorce her. On 19 July 1821, George's coronation day, Caroline was prevented from entering Westminster Abbey. Within nineteen days she had died and there were public riots on the occasion of her funeral.

As King, George became increasingly pro-Tory and also a valuable patron of the Arts. He died in 1830 aged sixty-seven, leaving no heirs, his only daughter Caroline having died in childbirth. He was succeeded by his brother, the Duke of Clarence, who became William IV.

They were a free and jovial race, but honest, brave, and true,
Who dipped their ladle in the punch when this old bowl was
new.

Oliver Wendell Holmes

The Clarence in Whitehall, London SW1, dating from 1862

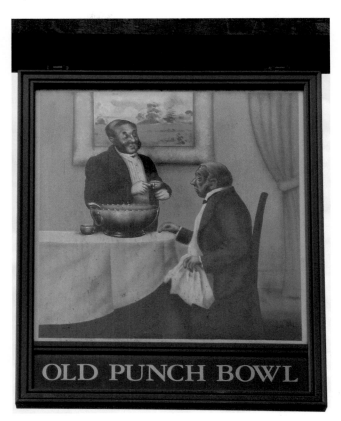

The Old Punch Bowl in Crawley, Sussex, halfway along the old London to Brighton mail coach route

preferred their bowl of punch, and displayed the sign of the Punch Bowl to welcome visiting party members to their towns and to warn unwelcome Tories.

The Whigs and Tories had their differences in drinking as well as politics. The Tories preferred claret and port, drinks produced by England's oldest allies, fortified by English vintners in Portugal to survive the voyage to England in the best possible condition. The Whigs

In June 1841 Henry Mayhew and Mark Lemon met in a London public house to discuss launching a satirical magazine. Some claim they met in the

The Punchbowl, *an eighteenth-century inn in Woodstock near Oxford*

The Punch Tavern, *London EC4*

Punch Tavern, then called the Crown & Sugar Loaf in Fleet Street, others that they met in the Edinburgh Castle in the Strand. Someone remarked that a good magazine, like a good bowl of punch, needed lemon, and *Punch* acquired its name. The first edition appeared the following month. Throughout some 160 years of publication *Punch*'s satirical articles and cartoons fought political battles, but became less radical over time as its early readers grew from rebellious youths into respectable middle-aged family men of Victorian Middle England.

The front cover portrayed Punch, the wife-beating glove puppet. Punch and Judy shows, originating in Italy, were held in nearby Ludgate Circus. His snozzle-voiced character also appears on the inn sign, and inside the Punch Tavern, renamed in the 1890s, copies of the magazine are on display.

Grandmother of Europe

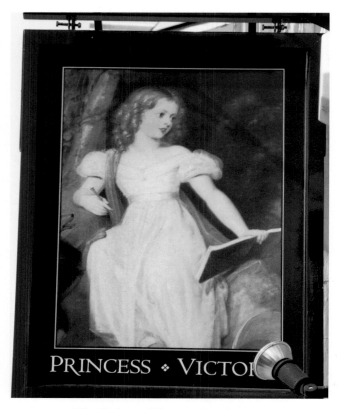

The Princess Victoria, London W8

On 24 May 1819, a daughter was born to the Duke of Kent. She was fifth in line to the throne, and few paid any attention to the Princess's birth, apart from the Prince Regent, whose own daughter had recently died. The Prince refused to let his niece be given a royal Christian name, but at the christening allowed the Archbishop of Canterbury to call her after her mother, Alexandrina Victoire. She became known as Victoria.

The sign of the Princess Victoria in Earl's Court Road, London, is taken from a painting by Richard Westall now known as *Queen Victoria as a Girl*. Her coronation in 1837 broke with the Hanoverian dynasty as Salic law prevented a woman becoming ruler of the German state if there was a male heir. Her uncle the Duke of Cumberland became King Ernest Augustus of Hanover and it became a separate entity until it was annexed by Prussia almost thirty years later.

A grade II listed building, named in honour of Queen Victoria's fourth daughter, is described in *The Good Pub Guide* as a splendid Victorian gin palace. *The London Pub* (2003) goes further, calling it "the finest, most complete, best-preserved, most authentic high-Victorian pub interior in London." Built in Holborn in 1872, and modified in 1891, with high ceilings and dark wooden furnishing, ornate windows, mirrors and

*The sign of **The Victoria** in Sleaford, Lincolnshire, does little for Her Majesty's regal image*

In 1840 the Queen married her cousin Prince Albert of Saxe-Coburg and Gotha. The bride and groom were both aged twenty. The marriage produced nine children and many grandchildren who would marry into the royal houses of Norway, Sweden, Denmark, Germany, Prussia, Russia, Greece, Spain and Yugoslavia and earn Victoria the epithet 'Grandmother of Europe'.

***The Princess Louise**, London WC1*

tiles, and a large front bar split off into cosy rooms and alcoves, it is a piece of England's history. The inn sign is based on a portrait of the Princess painted the year before the pub was built.

Born in 1848 as Louise Caroline Alberta, the Princess was an able sculptor and artist. After serving as unofficial secretary to her mother for five years, she married John Campbell, Marquis of Lorne, and they later became Duke and Duchess of Argyll. The Marquis was Governor General of Canada between 1873 and 1883. After his death in 1914 the Princess lived more or less as a recluse in Kensington Palace and died there childless in 1939 at the age of ninety-one. Named after her is the Canadian province of Alberta, an area five times the size of England.

Prince Albert died of typhoid at the age of forty (long before his daughter, Louise), and was mourned by the Queen for the rest of her life. She was determined his name should be preserved. Four years after he died, on the naming of her grandson, the future George V, she instructed her son, Albert, "Of course you will add Albert at the end, like your brothers. We settled long ago that all Papa's male descendants should bear our name to mark our line, just as I wish all the girls to have Victoria after theirs."

His portrait hangs outside a small stone-built pub in Church Street in the town of Ilkley, made famous by the Yorkshire anthem *On Ilkley Moor Bar T'at*, which reminds us of the dangers of venturing out onto the bleak moorland bareheaded.

The Albert, Ilkley

The Crystal Palace

The Crystal Palace *in Bath, built close to Bath Abbey in the year of the exhibition*

In the fifty years since 1800 Englishmen witnessed a phenomenal economic growth thanks to coal, iron and steam. No-one could see any future except peace and prosperity. Civil servant Henry Cole began to plan an exhibition to proclaim the nation's achievements to the world. The cosmopolitan Prince Albert supported his efforts and proposed that it should become "The Great Exhibition of the Works and Industry of All Nations". A Member of Parliament warned of the dangers to wives, daughters, property and health from hordes of foreigners invading London and bringing down the wrath of God.

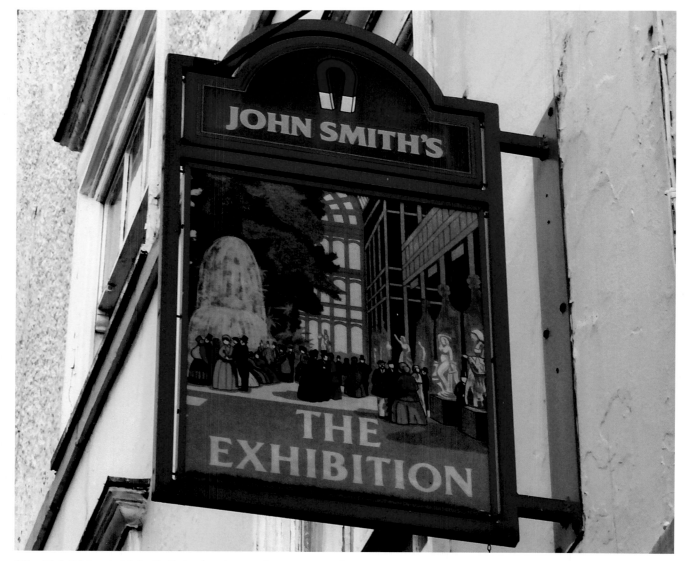

The Exhibition in York. Built in the nineteenth century as a large private house, it had become a hotel by 1872, having taken over the licence of an old inn opposite called the Bird in Hand, whose sign it displayed for the first few years. In 1879 the city's art gallery was built close by in Exhibition Square and the pub was renamed.

*The sign of **The Palace** in Leeds shows the interior of the exhibition. Once belonging to a boat-builder, the pub has long gardens extending to the River Aire and a long passage running from the cellars to the river.*

Nevertheless, the grand adventure went ahead to exhibit railway locomotives, marine engines and farm machinery, Macintosh's new rainwear, Goodyear's vulcanised rubber tyres, wrought iron household appliances and machines capable of producing eighty cigarettes a minute: thousands upon thousands of astonishing new products. Progress was hindered only by 250 designs for the venue being rejected. Joseph Paxton came to the rescue. He was the Duke of Devonshire's head gardener and his proposed design of cast iron and glass was based on the Duke's conservatory at Chatsworth House.

Three times the length of St Paul's Cathedral and 180 feet high to enclose three ancient elm trees, the exhibition centre was opened by Queen Victoria on 1 May 1851. During its construction *Punch* magazine nicknamed it 'The Crystal Palace'.

The Ploughman's Weary Way

The Plough in Museum Street, London WC1

The curfew tolls the knell of parting day
The lowing herd wind slowly o'er the lea
The ploughman homeward plods his weary way
And leaves the world to darkness and to me

Thomas Gray's *Elegy Written in a Country Churchyard*, published in 1751, takes us back to the old days of rural life. By this time England's population had reached about 5.7 million, back up to its level during Roman times and before the plagues of the fourteenth to sixteenth centuries. To expand, further agricultural development was needed and alongside the Industrial Revolution came the Agricultural Revolution. There were some inventions, such as the seed drill credited to Jethro Tull, but the main developments were achieved through selective breeding of livestock, forest clearances and crop rotation. Steam power became available thanks to

The Roseland Inn in the Cornish village of Philleigh. The rose-clad seventeenth-century inn's sign
was painted in 1982 by Stanley Chew, creator of some of England's most beautiful inn signs.

inventor James Watt, but the farmer still relied on horsepower for ploughing and moving his carts and wagons.

Since the use of firearms, the medieval Great Horse was no longer used to carry knights in armour and had retired to the farm. In the East Midlands it had been crossed with the Flemish horse to create the English shire horse, weighing more than a ton. In East Anglia the Suffolk Punch was bred. Chesnut in colour (in this breed's case the first 't' is omitted from the spelling), they are all descended from a single stallion foaled in the 1760s.

The Plough at Towcester, a 400-year-old pub on Watling Street, in the market square of Northamptonshire's oldest town

The Plough at Caunton, a Nottinghamshire village with a picturesque stream, Caunton Beck, well populated with families of ducks

Farm horses were taken care of by young unmarried men, contracted for a year at a time at hiring fairs and paid by board and lodge. When they had served their time they would usually marry and settle down as skilled farm labourers.

The plough has always been a popular inn sign, usually showing the old horse-drawn plough. For more than fifty years the national ploughing championships have been held at different venues in England, with one of the events being for the horse-drawn version.

The Wheatsheaf in Oxford, down an alleyway off the High Street. The inn has had its present name since 1761.

At harvest time, the whole village turned out to work up to sixteen hours a day to bring in the cereal crops. A staggered line of men, stripped to the waist and burnt by the midday sun, slashed with sickles and scythes. Stepping out of line spelt danger to life and limb from the grim reaper's sharp cutting tools. Women and children followed their menfolk, gathering in the corn and stacking it in the fields to

The Wheatsheaf in Shrewsbury, Shropshire

dry before bringing it under a thatched roof to store. During the Agricultural Revolution the comparatively low-yielding rye crops were replaced by wheat.

Many English inns bear the sign of The Wheatsheaf, usually in farming communities. However, the sign was often associated with bakers, the London Company of Bakers having three sheaves of wheat in their arms.

The Wheatsheaf, a town pub in King Street, Southwell, Nottinghamshire

In the centre of Ludlow stands a half-timbered building bearing the sign of Ye Olde Bullring Tavern. The English bullring was quite different from those in Spain, although the bull's fate in each of them would be similar. In the Middle Ages it was customary for butchers to place bulls in a ring and have them chased by dogs, in the belief that it would make the meat more tender. In fact, it had the opposite effect.

The Sheaf of Wheat, St Ives, Cornwall

Ye Olde Bullring Tavern, *Ludlow*

Before the eighteenth century most cattle and sheep were slaughtered before the onset of winter. There was little to feed them on through the cold months and their flesh provided welcome food for human consumption. This was changed by the farming of the humble turnip, which became widespread around 1750, feeding farmer and beast alike during the harsh winter. It also gave better crop rotation, and the livestock's winter manure added to the soil's fertility.

Robert Bakewell led experiments in cross-breeding of livestock from his Leicestershire farm. In 1750 he produced the Leicester sheep from the Lincoln and longhorn breeds, and in 1769 he produced a longhorn cattle breed, which gave a poor milk yield but a large quantity of meat. He was the first to breed livestock for their meat value and the first to hire out his animals for stud.

The records of London's Smithfield Market show that between 1710 and 1795 the average weight of sheep had risen from 38 to 80 pounds and the weight of cattle from 370 to 800 pounds. Many inns were named after cattle breeds and after massive individual animals. One of these was the celebrated Durham Ox, one of a docile breed introduced in the last quarter of the eighteenth century in County Durham, providing both beef and milk. It was acquired by John Day in 1802 when it was six years old and still growing. It reached five feet six inches tall, eleven feet long nose to tail and eleven feet in girth.

The Durham Ox, *Crayke*

Its sign is displayed outside a North Yorkshire village pub in Crayke. Converted from farm buildings, the Durham Ox was given the accolade of AA Pub of the Year for 2007-08. The sign's picture is from a print on display at the bar. It was dedicated by the artist to Lord Somerville, and public interest led to two thousand subscriptions for the print.

The stone-built Bull's Head in Castleton, Derbyshire, shows a Hereford Bull, bred in Herefordshire in 1742 by Benjamin Tomkins from a bull and two cows inherited from his father's estate. It was first exported to the USA in 1811. This docile animal is famous for its quality beef.

The Bull's Head, *Castleton*

The Bull Inn, *Southam*

The Bull Inn, *Little Walsingham*

The Bull Inn, an old coaching inn, stands on the old mail route between London and Birmingham in the Warwickshire market town of Southam. Its sign shows a white bull whose breed originates from the indigenous wild cattle of England, farmed by landowners for more than 800 years.

Another take on the origin of the sign of the Bull is a derivation from the Papal 'Bulla' (or the French 'La Boule'), the seal of a monastery or collegiate body. This might well be the case for The Bull Inn in the High Street of Little Walsingham, the Norfolk village of pilgrimages.

By 1800 English agriculture had grown to support a population of 10.8 million, and by 1850 one of 16.6 million. By that time the high output of crops was partly achieved through horse power and machinery; by 1850 only 22% of England's workforce was agricultural, the lowest proportion in the world.

The Spotted Ox *in the village of Tockwith, North Yorkshire*

***The Bull's Head**, outside the Warwickshire village of Little Alne*

The Museum

The Museum Tavern, London WC1

Since 1759 the British Museum has stood in London's Great Russell Street. It was originally established based on a huge collection of books, manuscripts, flora and scientific curios belonging to Sir Hans Sloane. Sir Hans was born in 1660 in Killyleagh, County Down, and moved to London to study a wide range of sciences. On his travels to Jamaica, as a physician, he collected 800 plant species. In 1693 he became secretary to the Royal Society, and later its president. He died in 1753 at the age of ninety-two, bequeathing his collection to a less than enthusiastic George II on behalf of the nation. However, Parliament intervened and the rest is history.

A portrait of Sir Hans, who gave his name to Sloane Square, hangs from the Museum Tavern on a corner opposite the museum. Originally the Dog & Duck, built on marshlands, the pub changed its name when the museum was built. Most of its fittings date from 1855 although the Victorian partitions have been taken down to make the interior much more light and airy. Its many visitors have included Winston Churchill, Karl Marx, J. B. Priestley and Dylan Thomas. Today's clientele include museum staff, taking a well-earned drink after their day's work, and visitors resting their weary legs or waiting here while books are delivered to their desks.

Although no longer to be seen near the museum, a sign of the Dog & Duck still hangs in Bateman Street in Soho. In Tudor times the district of Soho was the royal hunting ground and takes its name from the hunting call which once echoed across the fields. A plaque outside tells us that the Dog & Duck has been here since at least 1734 but that the existing building dates from 1897. It mentions George Orwell as a regular patron. The 2002 *Itchy Guide* described other patrons, old men with pipes in the corner. Sadly for some, under new laws the pipes have gone, but hopefully the old men will be there enjoying their beer for many years to come.

More often seen at inns near village ponds, the sign of the Dog and Duck relates to duck hunting, popular with King Charles II and lasting until the nineteenth century. Ducks with their wings clipped would be thrown into a pond and spaniels set upon them. The unfortunate ducks' only escape would be by diving below the surface.

The Dog & Duck, London W1

Prince Bertie

The King's Head, *Lichfield*

Queen Victoria and Prince Albert's eldest son was born in Buckingham Palace on 9 November 1841. Named Albert George, he was known for most of his life as Bertie. When Bertie's father died his mother virtually retired in mourning from public life but denied her son the opportunity to become involved in the government of the "Empire on which the sun never sets". In 1863 Bertie, then aged twenty-one, married eighteen-year-old Alexandra, daughter of King Christian IX of Denmark. Of their six children the eldest, Albert, died a week after his twenty-eighth birthday, leaving the future King George V as heir.

On Victoria's death on 22 January 1901, Bertie took the title King Edward VII, at fifty-nine the oldest man at that time to ascend the British throne. Edward and Alexandra were crowned King and Queen in Westminster Abbey on 9 August 1902.

His portrait, based on a full-length oil painting by Sir Samuel Luke Fildes painted in the coronation year, hangs outside Lichfield's oldest pub, The King's Head. The inn claims to date from 1408. A plaque outside tells us that "Colonel Luke Lillingston raised a regiment of Foot at the King's Head on 25 March 1705" and gives a short history of what became the South Staffordshire regiment.

The King's chosen career would have been in the army. He served briefly with the Grenadier Guards in 1861, rising rapidly to the rank of colonel, but as heir to the throne he was not allowed to see active service. Nevertheless he did involve himself in the reorganisation of the Army Medical Service.

His civilian portrait hangs outside a public house named in his honour in York's Nunnery Lane, overlooking the city walls. The Edward VII had been licensed as a beerhouse in 1863, but did not acquire a full licence until 1901, the year Edward became King. A few doors away are the Victoria Vaults, named in memory of his mother.

The portrait is from another oil painting by Fildes. A mirror image, by the same artist, was presented to the Fellows of King's College Hospital in 1906. The King had been elected to an honorary fellowship of the college in 1897 while still Prince of Wales. He opened a new wing of the London Hospital and laid the foundation stones for three others. King Edward died on 6 May 1910 at Sandringham, after a series of heart attacks. He is buried in St George's Chapel in Windsor Castle.

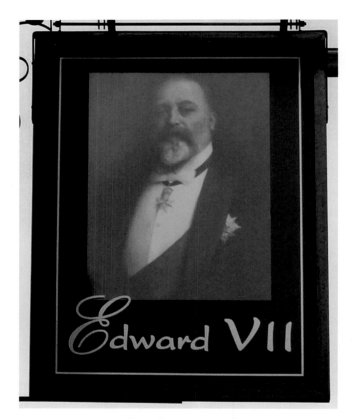

The Edward VII, York

A Cure for All Ills

St Christopher Inn, Bath, *formerly* **The Oliver**

In Green Street in Bath stands a pub which reopened in 2003 as a backpackers' hostel, named the St Christopher Inn after the patron saint of travellers. Above the corner doorway it still displays its old sign 'The Oliver', and the legend below the cameo reads: "Dr Oliver, inventor, 1735 registered trade mark."

Dr William Oliver helped to create the Mineral Hospital in Bath, once the Roman city of Aqua Sulis and famed for its spa waters for almost two thousand years. Dr Oliver was the hospital's chief physician for more than twenty years. An authority on gout, he is perhaps best remembered for his invention of the Bath Oliver biscuit as a recommended diet for overweight patients.

In 1962, when The Oliver opened, the *Bath Chronicle* reported that Oliver had given the recipe to his coachman, Atkins, who had set up shop here almost exactly 200 years before.

In the eighteenth century bathing for cleanliness was becoming popular and by Victorian times the middle classes believed that one had to be clean to be respectable. An Act of Parliament in 1846 ordered towns to provide bathing facilities for the poor. The rhyme of a popular song of the time went:

> *There's comfort coming, goodness knows*
> *For poor folks and their spouses.*
> *They can wash their persons and their clothes*
> *In baths and washing houses.*

Hales Bar, *Harrogate*

The north of England's equivalent to Bath's spa waters are in the Yorkshire town of Harrogate. Inside Hales Bar, which claims to be the town's oldest and most historic inn, the history of the spa, and of the inn, is displayed. It tells how the premises in Crescent Road go back to when sulphur wells were discovered in the mid-seventeenth century: sulphur and springs still flow beneath the cellar and their distinctive odours occasionally percolate up to the bar area.

It was once a successful coaching inn on the trans-Pennine mail coach route from York to Preston. Rebuilt at the end of the coaching era, it took its present name in 1882 when William Hales became landlord. The main bar retains many of its Victorian features, with memorabilia including hunting trophies and glass cases of stuffed birds. Used by Sir John Barbirolli as his favourite bar when the Halle Orchestra visited to play in the town, it was also used for interior scenes in the film *Chariots of Fire*.

The Flask in Hampstead, London NW3, built on the site of an older inn called the Thatched House, which was demolished in 1874. The old inn was built in the fields on the site of a spring and supplied flasks of water to the expanding suburbs of London.

Looking back in time, one can understand the value of good quality water. In 1854 the world's third cholera pandemic took the lives of 10,738 Londoners. The first, in 1832, was responsible for fifty-five thousand deaths in Britain and the second, in 1849, killed more than fourteen thousand in London alone.

It was thought that the disease was caused by bad air rising from the sewers, but Dr John Snow had a different theory. Snow had been born in York in 1813 and apprenticed to a surgeon at the age of fourteen. He moved to London in 1836 and by 1850 had been admitted to the Royal College of Surgeons. He had mapped the spread of the disease and traced many cases to the water pump in Broad Street (now Broadwick Street). He found that the pump had been contaminated by sewage from a cesspit at house number 40. He concluded that cholera was spread by infected water, although it was almost fifty years before the world was convinced.

Dr Snow was also a renowned anaesthetist and administered chloroform to Queen Victoria as she gave birth to two of her children, Leopold and Beatrice. He died of a stroke in 1858.

The John Snow, London W1

Number 39 Broadwick Street was licensed as the Newcastle-upon-Tyne in 1721. For some years it was the local of William Blake, artist and visionary, who set up an engraver's shop at number 27 in 1784. The pub was rebuilt in 1867, and in 1954, on the centenary of Snow's discovery, it was renamed in his honour. A plaque outside tells us "The red granite kerbstone marks the site of the historic Broad Street Pump associated with Dr John Snow's discovery in 1854 that cholera is conveyed by water."

Since medieval times the sign of the barber-surgeon has been a red and white pole representing a limb swathed in bandages. Many such signs can still be seen today outside hairdressers' shops.

An ornate-fronted Victorian pub in London's Chinatown displays the intriguing sign of The Crooked Surgeon. The building, in Lisle Street, was home to St John's Hospital for Diseases of the Skin between 1935 and the 1980s.

The pub is named after John Laws Milton, member of the Royal College of Surgeons, born in Bishopwearmouth in 1820 and founder of the hospital in 1863. Although described as brilliant, he was also controversial and was said to have abused his position by running a lucrative private clinic in the hospital, then located in Leicester Square, for treatment of non-existent diseases.

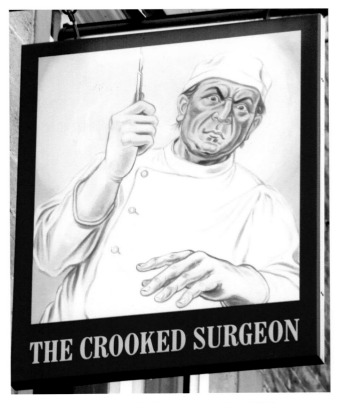

***The Crooked Surgeon**, London WC2*

The nursing profession has its foundations far away in the Turkish town of Scutari. It was here that Florence Nightingale founded her hospital for the wounded British soldiers of the Crimean War. Britain, France and the kingdom of Sardinia had united with Turkey to stifle Russian imperial expansion. Alfred, Lord Tennyson's famous *Charge of the Light Brigade* commemorates the action at Balaclava, in modern-day Ukraine:

Cannon to right of them,
Cannon to left of them,
Cannon in front of them
Volley'd and thunder'd
Storm'd at with shot and shell,
Boldly they rode and well
Into the jaws of Death,
Into the mouth of Hell
Rode the six hundred

His poem tells how, on 25 October 1854, 673 cavalrymen were sent on a three-quarter mile charge to their fate through bungled orders exchanged by army officers who were not on speaking terms. There is a story that Captain Nolan, at the head of the charge, was decapitated by a cannonball, but his body remained in the saddle, convincing the gunners that the brigade was being led by a headless demon.

A month earlier, the first significant battle of the war took place when the allied forces crossed the steep banks of the heavily defended River Alma. So confident had the Russians been that rich citizens had set up family picnics on the heights overlooking the river to watch their army's success. Many of them may have suffered from indigestion as they hurried to leave the scene.

The sign of the Alma in Cambridge shows a British soldier standing over destroyed artillery, possibly the bronze guns of Sevastopol from which Victoria Crosses, Britain's highest military award, have always been made.

Four days before the battle of Balaclava, Florence Nightingale had set out for the war zone with a team of twenty-eight women volunteers. At the military hospital in Scutari the conditions they found were horrific. Florence, named after her Italian birthplace, became known as 'The Lady with the Lamp' as she tended the wounded soldiers by night, carrying her pet owl in her pocket. Her time in Scutari took its toll and, having contracted many illnesses, she was almost at death's door the following year. Her collapse from exhaustion in August 1857 signalled the effective end of her nursing career but she lived on to the age of ninety, dying on 13 October 1910 of old age. Her work led to the founding of the Nightingale Fund for training nurses. The legacy of her work continues to this day at King's College in London.

The Alma, Cambridge

A War to End All Wars

The Edith Cavell, *Norwich*

The Edith Cavell is a single-roomed corner pub close to Norwich Cathedral and the nurse's monument. It opened as a bar in 1981, having been the Army and Navy Stores for more than a hundred years.

Born 4 December 1865 in the nearby village of Swardeston, Edith was the daughter of the local vicar. She spent many years as a trained nurse in England and Belgium and in her early forties was in charge of a pioneering nursing school in Brussels. During the First World War the school was in occupied territory, and from here she organised the escape of British soldiers back to England. Exposed by a Belgian collaborator, she was arrested by the German military and executed by firing squad in the early hours of 12 October 1915. Her last words were: "Standing, as I do, in the view of God and eternity, I realise that patriotism is not enough. I must have no hatred or bitterness towards anyone."

Allied war propaganda made her a national heroine. After the war, her body was taken to Westminster Abbey for the first part of a funeral ceremony before being buried in Norwich close to the pub that bears her name.

Stands the church clock at ten to three?
And is there honey still for tea?

Rupert Brooke's final lines from *The Vicarage, Granchester* reflect peaceful rural England in 1912. The local inn, a few miles to the south-west of Cambridge, is named after the young poet, who lived nearby. Its sign shows the clock still at ten minutes to three, and the inn's timber beams and log fires hark back to the tranquillity of a century ago.

Two years later the serenity was broken by the outbreak of war. On his way to fight, the poet was taken ill and died on a hospital ship aged only twenty-seven, on St George's Day 1915. This son of a Rugby School housemaster lies buried in an olive grove in a remote part of the Aegean island of Scyros, where his ship had been anchored. He left us his moving poem *The Soldier*, which begins:

If I should die think only this of me:
That there's some corner of a foreign field
That is forever England.

The Rupert Brooke, *Granchester*

Index of Inns

bold text indicates illustrations.

Index of People

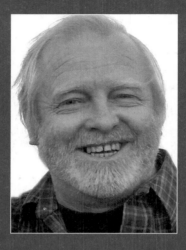

Pete Coxon was born in Middlesbrough in 1947. Married with a son and two daughters, he now lives in York.

After a career in finance, he has spent much of his time writing and illustrating.

Pete is passionate about unearthing history and has explored the lives and times of his ancestors back to Tudor times.

An active member of York Art Society and until recently the editor of its quarterly magazine, he has sold several paintings at exhibitions.

Over the last few years he has been a regular contributor to the *Good Pub Guide* and is a member of the Inn Sign Society.

His first book, *York's Historic Inns,* is the story of a city and its people woven around its inns and public houses. His second *Landlords and Rogues* gives an anecdotal account of 19th century life.

Pete has spent much of his time recently travelling throughout England and many other countries. His latest work, **The Hart of England**, describes English life, history and culture, illustrated throughout by photographs of inn signs taken on his travels.